COASTAL GEORGIA

GOLDEN COAST PUBLISHING CO.

1. PALMETTO
2. LIGHTHOUSE, CA. 1840, LITTLE CUMBERLAND ISLAND

COASTAL GEORGIA

PHOTOGRAPHY BY VAN JONES MARTIN WITH TEXT BY BETH LATTIMORE REITER

First Printing.

ISBN 0-932958-02-8

ISBN 0-932958-03-6 pbk.

Library of Congress Card
Catalog No. 85-81036

Copyright 1985 by The Coastal
Highway District of Georgia.

 Coastal Georgia has been published at the
initiative of the Coastal Area Planning and
Development Commission, Brunswick,
Georgia.

Produced and distributed by
Golden Coast Publishing Co.,
22 Waite Drive, Savannah, Georgia 31406.
Telephone, (912) 352-2385.

Designed and produced by Lisa Lytton.

Typesetting by DG&F Typography,
Columbia, South Carolina.

Color separations by Savannah Color
Separations, Savannah, Georgia.

Rights to use photographs shared with the
Coastal Area Planning and Development
Commission of Georgia.

Rights to photograph on page 1 retained by
Tourist Division, Georgia Department of
Industry and Trade.

Rights to photographs on pages 62 top, 68
all, 72 top, 85, 88 all, 105, 109 retained by
Van Jones Martin. Rights to photograph on
page 108 top retained by Marion Fleming
Martin III.

ACKNOWLEDGMENTS

Several years ago I began collecting material and taking photographs with the hope that some day they could be used in the production of a book on coastal Georgia. Coincidentally, in Brunswick, Vernon Martin, executive director of the Coastal Area Planning and Development Commission, was gathering resources and support to publish such a book. Since that time he has been unwavering in his persistence and dedication to this goal, and through his efforts this book has become a reality.

The Coastal Highway District, which has been instrumental in the realization of so many worthy dreams of coastal organizations, graciously gave a matching grant to get the book out of the planning stage and into production. Serving on this vitally important committee are: Chairman Ed Garvin, Tourism Committee Chairman Charles Davis, E. Ralph Bufkin, Willie Brown, Robert P. Miller, Dr. W. E. Smith, Charles M. Jones, Franklin Crandall, George L. Hannaford, and P. H. Ploeger.

Governor Joe Frank Harris, convinced of the long-range contribution of this book to the documentation and promotion of the living history of Georgia, made funds available that were crucial to the successful completion of this project. State Senator Glenn Bryant of Hinesville and state Representative Larry Walker of Perry were instrumental in obtaining funding support from the Governor.

I owe a sincere debt of gratitude to Beth Reiter and to Lisa Lytton. Beth wrote a wonderful text under the exasperating publishing pressures of time and space, and Lisa patiently retained the integrity of her original designs while I kept adding more photographs and text.

There have been numerous others who have contributed in many ways in this long and complicated process, by helping me with the photographs and excerpts and aiding Beth in her research for the text. I would like to extend a blanket of thanks to this diverse group of individuals—without their help the production of *Coastal Georgia* would have been an impossible task.

At the CAPDC: Judi Morgan and Kathleen Durham were cheerfully indispensable—Judi in the beginning when we were trying to get off the ground, and Kathleen near the end when we were trying to land safely.

The Georgia Department of Natural Resources: former Commissioner Joe D. Tanner, Game and Fish Division Director Leon Kirkland, Captain Paul Leverett, Sergeant Tom Lane, Corporal Bill Haley, Corporal Homer Bryson, Ranger Mark Padgett, Mr. and Mrs. C. V. Waters, David Edwards, Gene Love, Richard Daigle, Daniel Brown, and Margaret Melton.

The U. S. District Corps of Engineers; the Georgia Historical Society; the Savannah-Chatham Public Library; the State Historic Preservation Office; and the Massie Heritage Interpretation Center.

Interested friends and folks: Bill Thompson; Clermont Lee; Ty Potterfield; Dan Brown and Talley Kirkland at Fort Pulaski; Phil Flournoy; Bob Busby; Hank Ramsey; Jimmy and Rachel Vann; Bill Haynes; Alex Gilmore; Bud Frankenthaler; Harry Chapman; Gloria Harrison; Jenny Stacy; Eloise Bailey; Gertrude Lark; Norman V. Turner; Anne Shelander; Jack Helmuth; Dr. and Mrs. James F. Gowen and family.

At Savannah Color Separations: David Kaminsky and Betsy Cain; Rusty Smith; Bob Holladay; and Sarah Sowell. Family: Beth's husband, John Reiter, and her mother, Mildred Lattimore; Jerry and Julie Martin and family; my Aunt Dar; my brother, Fleming; and my parents, Marion and Kate Martin, who have always encouraged me.

Finally, I would like to thank Barbara, who typed the manuscript, listens patiently while I bounce ideas around, seems always willing to look at another bunch of slides, and has stuck by me through thin and thin.

Van Jones Martin, July 15, 1985

3. WIRE-GRASS

TABLE OF CONTENTS

4. CAT-TAIL

5. WILD AZALEA

6. PINE

INTRODUCTION

On U. S. Highway 17, one enters Georgia from the north by crossing the Savannah River. Between the Savannah and the St. Marys River to the south, this coastal road cuts a 110-mile avenue through the heart of a land of wild beauty and fascinating history. Within the pages of this book the reader will find that in some ways, not much has changed in the 4,500 years since Indians began to hunt in the oak and pine forests and fish the bountiful rivers of this region. The environment weaves its way into the lives of those who come here and leaves its imprint on the soul. It affects the diet, culture, commerce, and even the temperament of the most worldly traveler.

> "To be short, it is a thing unspeakable to consider the things that bee seene there, and shal be founde more and more in this incomparable land, which never yet broken with plough yrons, bringeth forth all things according to his first nature wherewith the eternall God indued it. ...(It is) the fairest, fruitfullest, and pleasantest of all the world."
>
> *Captain Jean Ribault, 1562*

The first Europeans to explore the waters of this coast were awed by the verdant subtropical landscape, and their reports were filled with fantastic descriptions of the natural abundance of vegetation, game, and seafood. Of course, the Indians who had been living in this area for centuries already knew this. The huge prehistoric heaps of discarded oyster shells offer conclusive evidence that the marshes and rivers generously supplied them with their needs. They no doubt thought that there was enough to share with the white man.

But the Spanish and then the British subverted the Indians' ways and eventually drove them from the region. The English came with high ideals— to establish a colony of hardworking individual farmers, men and women who were without hope in their homeland, but would prosper in a world of new opportunities.

The crops that were ideally suited for this region, however, were best produced under a system of large plantations, and the dreams of the Trustees were never realized. In fact, the planters who were most successful were the leaders in the radical movement for independence.

After the Revolution the economy of coastal Georgia continued to ride on the back of agriculture. The port cities prospered as the cultivation of rice and cotton increased. But the economy had a soft underbelly—the investment of capital in slave labor. The Civil War ended that era, and the merchants looked elsewhere for commodities to trade.

Interestingly, the "crop" that fueled the coastal economy after the demise of the plantation system was the timber—oak, pine, and cypress—that had been cleared in the past to make way for fields of cotton and rice. The lumber production of the Georgia coast was phenomenal, and the ports of Savannah, Darien, Brunswick, and St. Marys reaped the benefits of its trade.

As transportation and communication technology improved, the islands became more accessible, and tourism became the next great industry of the region. The post Civil War restoration and expansion of the railroads was the first step in accommodating the travelers who had begun to read about the charms of the golden coast. The completion of the great Atlantic highway through Georgia, however, was the real catalyst in the tourist boom, and the newly autonomous travelers began to require more and better facilities for their enjoyment.

Golf courses and tennis courts were constructed to supplement the natural amenities of the coast, and the modern picture was almost complete. Progress and population began to threaten the very historic and environmental landmarks that visitors were coming to see, until groups of citizens began to form organizations for the protection of these treasures. The resulting preservation movement has been a huge success.

The oyster shell middens of prehistoric Indians may still be seen on coastal islands. The ruins of the colonial Frederica are maintained for modern discovery. The City of Savannah is a marvel unto itself—its meticulously planned system of avenues and squares has been preserved for contemporary enjoyment and habitation. Millionaires' Village on Jekyll Island is a monument to the greatest single conservation tool to benefit the Georgia coast—the acquisitive powers of northern industrial wealth. The Cumberland Island National Seashore continues to awe visitors with its natural majesty.

In the following pages, an informative text, vivid accounts of historical events, and heartfelt impressions of the natural arena present the story of this region through a variety of viewpoints, from the age of European exploration to the contemporary movement for historic and environmental preservation. The accompanying photographs illustrate the timeless splendor of the coastal landscape and the charm and diversity of its historic sites. These chronicles, however clever, can only describe this wonderful place. To truly understand the magic of the Georgia coast, one must experience it—smell the thick salt air, feel the beach sand underfoot, listen to the calming ocean waves, witness the sun setting over the broad marshes, and taste the catch of the day—then the image becomes complete, and the impressions will last a lifetime.

The Prehistoric Coast

A rising and falling ocean level has dramatically shaped and reshaped the coastline of Georgia through the centuries. Landlocked bluffs and ridges, once a part of a prehistoric barrier island system, formed healthy locations for cities such as Savannah and sites for breezy summer retreats like the Ridge near Darien. Other sand ridges formed by ancient ocean waves provided the easiest arteries for Indian trails. White settlers later adapted and expanded these trails, which subsequently became the basis of modern road systems.

The barrier islands that extend the length of the Georgia coast shield the mainland from the erosive action of wind, waves, and tidal surges. The waterways behind these islands provide a protected, scenic inland passage. Although much of the present coastline was formed 40,000 years ago—a relatively short time in geological history—portions of the coast have been in the making only for the past 5,000 years. Williamson Island to the south of Wassaw Island has appeared in the last twenty-five years. Dynamic changes to the seacoast may be noticed on a yearly basis, and current shifts and storm driven waves can alter the shoreline in a single season. Therefore, while some houses have been moved back from the encroaching sea several times since the nineteenth century, other seacoast areas have reestablished dune systems and regained lost beaches.

Human occupation of the islands occurred as early as 2500 B.C., and fiber-tempered pottery shards from this period are among the earliest found in any part of North America. The fertile marshes and estuaries and abundant animal life supported human subsistence. Flushed by tidal currents, the marshes nurture clams, whelks, shrimp, and crabs. Vast trash heaps of empty oyster shells, called shell middens, indicate that oysters were a staple in prehistoric diets, and these mounds of discarded shells were so numerous that European settlers used them as the principal ingredient in the invention of a durable building material called tabby.

Although the saber-toothed tiger and other prodigious beasts once roamed the prehistoric coastal forests, more docile creatures have supplied man with diverse hunting opportunities in recent centuries. Not as numerous as when they provided food for the tables of early settlers, deer, marsh rabbits, and raccoons still wander across island lawns. Wild turkeys and hogs continue to survive on the less settled islands and in many mainland forests. Dragonlike alligators, which sunned themselves on primeval river banks, were only recently endangered by zealous hunters. Now protected, their numbers are increasing, and it is not unusual to see one lounging beside a golf lagoon. Native and migratory birds teem on the beaches and in the marshes, swamps, and forests. Egrets, osprey, herons, marsh hens, and even the bald eagle may be seen in much the same habitats that existed in prehistoric times. Some species, however, have not withstood the challenge of man. The exotic Carolina parrots, for example, no longer flash through coastal forests.

Plentiful native foods, including persimmon, black cherries, grapes, blueberries, blackberries, and palm fruit, give credence to reports of early travelers about finding a land of tropical plenty. The islands that were for centuries the hunting and fishing grounds for nomadic Indians would eventually attract the eye of imperial Europe. The stage was set for colonization.

The First Europeans

Explorers and seekers of fortune plied the sea along the coast of Georgia as early as the fifteenth century. Jean Ribault, a sixteenth-century French explorer, took enough notice of this coast to compliment its beauty and to give its rivers short-lived French names. It was Spain, however, which claimed title to the territory between the Savannah and St. Marys rivers in the sixteenth century, and the Spanish were the first Europeans to spend any significant period of time on the coast. In 1566, Spanish monks of the Jesuit order established several missions on the coastal islands, but they were forced to withdraw by Indian hostilities after only a few years.

The mission efforts of the Franciscan order were somewhat more successful, although tensions with the Indians never entirely ceased during Spanish occupation. The missions appear to have been built as much for political purposes as for religious ones. The settlements provided an impediment to other European colonization and served as centers to civilize and control the Indian population.

Muskogean-speaking Indians occupied the central coast when the Spanish arrived on the shores of the Georgia territory. The Spanish called them Guale. These Indians had a social order, and, like their prehistoric predecessors, were a seasonal, seminomadic people. St. Catherines Island was the capital of their nation and also the site of the mission Santa Catalina de Guale, currently the focus of intensive archaeological investigation.

Although monks christianized some Indians, more often the natives rebelled at attempts to convert them. In the long run, however, this collision with the Europeans shattered the social order of the Indians. New diseases, from which they had no immunity, decimated their numbers, and gradually, but inevitably, they were forced further and further inland.

In the seventeenth century, the many inlets, creeks, and rivers of coastal Georgia offered perfect hideaways for the pirates who preyed on Spanish and English shipping lines. The English despised pirates and accorded them no rights by English law. One of the most infamous who reputedly prowled the Georgia coast was Edward Teach, an English privateer-turned-pirate. Called Blackbeard, he looped slow-burning hemp in his plaited hair and terrorized ships in a most deadly manner. Blackbeard was finally put to death in hand-to-hand combat by Lieutenant Robert Maynard of His Majesty's *Pearl* in 1718, and Blackbeard Island, now a national wildlife refuge, is the legendary location of his pirate treasure, supposedly kept watch over by the devil himself.

The coast of Georgia became a hotly disputed territory in the late-seventeenth century. The Carolinians feared Indian uprisings, renewed Spanish imperialism, and encirclement by the French from the west. They petitioned England to settle frontier towns and forts to defend their southern border and prevent interruption of their lucrative trade with the interior. England responded with a plan to establish a fort at the mouth of the Altamaha River. This fort was ultimately built at the expense and initiative of Carolina in 1721. Known as Fort King George, the site was unhealthy and unpopular with the garrison, and it was abandoned in 1727. Carolina, however, continued to petition London with suggestions for other frontier towns.

Colonization

While defense and Indian trade concerned Carolinians, the humanitarian and philanthropic origins of the colony of Georgia were fermenting in London. In 1729, James Edward Oglethorpe was appointed to head a committee of Parliament to investigate the condition of English prisons. The committee found these prisons in miserable condition, occupied for the most part by debtors, not criminals. Oglethorpe met Dr. Thomas Bray, a philanthropist also interested in prison reform and founder of the Society for the Propagation of the Gospel in Foreign Parts. From this acquaintance grew the proposal for establishing a charity colony south of the Carolinas.

Shortly thereafter, on February 12, 1733, Oglethorpe settled a permanent colony at Savannah. Ironically, among the 114 passengers who made the first voyage, not more than a dozen were debtors, and there were no professional soldiers other than Oglethorpe. The initial settlers were principally modest tradesmen and a few gentlemen who paid their own way. The 1732 charter of Georgia allowed a free exercise of religion for all settlers except Roman Catholics, and this provision became a significant attraction for several groups of Europeans. The first colonists were soon joined by a succession of persecuted protestants, such as the German Salzburgers who settled up the Savannah River in Effingham County at a town named Ebenezer.

Jews were permitted to settle in Savannah in July 1733. Although many Sephardic families moved on to Charleston when Georgia was drawn into war between England and Spain, several families, including the Minis and Sheftalls, remained in the Savannah community. Other families later joined them, and many distinguished themselves in the Continental Army. The congregation Mickve Israel was formed in 1735 and continues to hold services, presently in a handsome gothic revival synagogue constructed in 1876.

One of the basic reasons for establishing the Georgia colony was to experiment with the growing of medicinal herbs. In addition, it was hoped that through the cultivation of grapes and mulberry trees, wine and silk industries would hasten the economic stability of the colony. A public nursery was established at Savannah in 1733, and orange trees from southern Europe were planted. Apple, pear, peach, and other fruit trees were also planted, however, many varieties were not successful. Although citrus trees will grow for several seasons during mild winters, the occasional hard freezes that do occur along the coast made much of what was planted in the garden impractical. The ten-acre Trustees' Garden gradually ceased as an enterprise, but experimental gardening on private plantations flourished in the botanically rich coastal plain of Georgia well into the nineteenth century. Wormsloe, a significant land grant estate of Noble Jones on Isle of Hope in Chatham County, served as a testing garden for mulberry trees and grape vines.

The Leadership of James Edward Oglethorpe

The remarkable town plan that Oglethorpe developed for Savannah followed a typical grid pattern of streets, but many distinctive characteristics distinguished it among Colonial planned towns. The numerous green squares in Savannah repeated in harmony with the original plan each time the city expanded from 1733 until 1856, are perhaps its most outstanding feature. Each colonist received a sixty by ninety-foot town lot, which was grouped in parcels of ten, known as a tything, around a central open square. Four tythings constituted a ward, which, together with the square, was the basic neighborhood building block of the plan. In addition, each colonist received a five-acre garden lot and a forty-five acre farm lot beyond the precincts of the city. Open lands to the east, west, and south of the city were retained by the inhabitants for future growth. Miraculously, each time Savannah expanded the city fathers chose to imitate the original plan. The twenty-one surviving squares are a model of city planning, cooling the city in summer and tempering modern traffic flow.

As part of Oglethorpe's plan, and in an effort to maintain a colony of small diverse farms, no colonist was to receive greater than five hundred acres of land outside of the city commons. This was in direct contrast to the large landholdings permitted in South Carolina which required slave labor to work.

Slavery was forbidden in Georgia, however, and large plantations would have been impractical. The Trustees felt that slave labor might corrupt the work ethics of the industrious independent farmers they were trying to encourage, and also feared the addition of a potentially rebellious element in an already exposed frontier position.

Oglethorpe encountered a small band of Creek Indians on Yamacraw Bluff. Tomochichi, mico of the tribe, befriended Oglethorpe and even traveled with him to England. On Tomochichi's death, the venerable chief was buried in the center of Wright Square with Oglethorpe serving as one the pallbearers. Seven minute guns and three volleys of small arms were fired as his body was laid to rest.

Oglethorpe succeeded in obtaining land cessions from the Creeks which extended the Georgia territory to the Altamaha River. Securing the defenses of Georgia along the frontier was of immediate concern to Oglethorpe, and to that end he established a series of satellite settlements along the coast. A group of Highland Scots renowned for their fighting ability settled New Inverness, later called Darien, on the Darien River in 1736. They mounted their guns on the ruins of Fort King George and formed a stalwart military force.

That same year Oglethorpe created another frontier base of operations against the Spanish on St. Simons Island. On the western side of the island, he laid out a fort and a thirty-five-acre walled town called Frederica. This incursion south of the Altamaha went unchallenged by the Indians, but greatly infuriated the Spanish. In 1742, the Spanish attacked St. Simons and, although heavily outnumbered, Oglethorpe succeeded in repulsing the attack at the Battle of Bloody Marsh. In so doing, he helped blunt the desires of Spain for northward expansion and continued the pattern of Anglo-American Colonial growth.

The inhabitants of Frederica were principally artisans and tradesmen who depended on the presence of the regiment for much of their livelihood. With the reduction of the Spanish threat, the regiment was withdrawn and the citizens of Frederica began to drift away in search of work elsewhere. Shortly after 1749, Frederica ceased to function as a community. Its tabby ruins still stand as the only tangible evidence of its existence.

Restrictions Are Lifted and the Colony Prospers

In fact, the entire colony of Georgia was losing population at this time, shrinking dramatically from about five thousand persons to five hundred. Part of the reason lay in the Trustees' strict land policies that leased land in Tail Male. Under this provision, there was no outright ownership of land and female inheritence of property was prohibited. Lands could not be mortgaged or sold. These restrictions, combined with the prohibition against slavery, greatly hampered the economic development of the colony. Disgruntled colonists known as the "Malcontents" began applying pressure for change.

In 1752, the Georgia charter was resigned to the Crown. Under the provincial government, Royal governors were able to make fee simple grants giving colonists clear title to their lands. In an effort to rebuild the prosperity of the province, the Crown offered grants of land to individuals who would improve the land for agricultural or commercial endeavors within three years. Such inducements attracted new settlers to the colony. Five thousand grants from this period are recorded.

In 1758, seven parishes, which served as political and religious subdivisions, were created. The seat of the provincial government was located at Savannah in Christ Church Parish. In 1763, the English Crown extended its southern boundary (without a treaty with the Indians) to the St. Marys River, and four more parishes were created.

The prohibition of slavery was also lifted in 1752, finally allowing the economic exploitation of a tremendous coastal resource. The slow moving channels of inland swamp streams could be dammed and controlled to provide irrigation for the production of rice. This gravity flow system, which had its origins in the southeast about 1724, was ideal for the swamps along the creeks and tributaries of the Ogeechee, Canoochee, Midway, and Newport rivers. The monumental task of swamp clearing, dam building, and channel digging would never have been attempted, however, without the introduction of the newest member of the increasing culturally diverse family of Georgia—the African slave.

In 1752, a new era of growth began when Puritan settlers from the Beach Hill and Dorchester communities in South Carolina arrived with their slaves in what is now the Midway District. These Midway settlers had made their way to South Carolina from Massachusetts. Many distinguished ministers served this community, including Abiel Holmes, the father of the celebrated author Oliver Wendell Holmes, Sr., and grandfather of Oliver Wendell Holmes, Jr., the U. S. Supreme Court Chief Justice. Jedidiah Morse, the father of Samuel F. B. Morse, also served Midway. Sons of Midway also went on to become distinguished public servants, including three U. S. senators, four Georgia governors, a North Carolina governor, and the first U. S. minister to China and Japan.

Mark Carr received a land grant in 1752 of five hundred acres at the mouth of the Midway River. In 1758, he conveyed three hundred acres to several Midway settlers for the express purpose of establishing a convenient seaport for the rice planters. Sunbury prospered, and by 1770 was said to be the rival of Savannah in port activity.

The Revolution in Georgia

In spite of her rice exports, Georgia, the youngest of the American colonies, was also the poorest just prior to the Revolution. Lacking an industrial base to produce consumer goods, Georgia imported more than she exported, and, sparsely populated, she needed to rely on the protection of England to man her frontiers. It is understandable then why Georgians were reluctant to get caught up in the events leading to the Revolution.

Georgia did react to the Intolerable Acts (which closed the port of Boston) by calling a meeting of parishes in 1774. Although the meeting called for redress, the gathering rejected the idea of sending delegates to the First Continental Congress in Philadelphia. The conservative element that dominated the meeting was made up of older Georgians with close personal and economic ties to England. The parishes of St. Johns and St. Andrews, however, populated by fiery Scots and independent-thinking New England Congregationalists, did not share this conservative viewpoint. The inhabitants of the Midway District called a separate meeting and assigned Lyman Hall, a large landholder, to represent St. Johns Parish in Philadelphia. Fearing that he would not be seated since he did not represent the whole colony, he did not attend.

St. Johns Parish soon after called for all parishes to adopt a boycott of British trade. St. Andrews Parish (Darien) eagerly adopted the boycott, but few other parishes followed suit. St. Johns Parish grew more and more impatient with the moderate tone that Georgia was taking and even petitioned to be annexed to South Carolina, but the offer was politely refused.

Lyman Hall was again named the delegate from St. Johns Parish to the Second Continental Congress. He made the long journey with 150 barrels of rice and fifty pounds sterling for the relief of the blockaded citizens of Boston. He was admitted to the Congress, but he would not vote since again he did not represent the entire colony. In July 1776, when the Continental Congress adopted the Declaration of Independence, Georgia was represented by three signers. It is not surprising that two of the three, Lyman Hall and Button Gwinnett, were residents of St. Johns Parish. Coincidentally, the third signer, George Walton, was later held prisoner at Sunbury after being captured by the British at Savannah.

The old parish system of government was replaced by a county system in 1777. Chatham County was named for William Pitt, the earl of Chatham and prime minister of England. Effingham was named for Lord Effingham, friend of the American colonies who resigned his commission in the British army when ordered to serve in America. Camden was named for Charles Pratt, earl of Camden and lord chancellor of England. Glynn was named for John Glynn, member of Parliament and friend of the colonists. Liberty, created from St. Johns and St. Andrews parishes, was appropriately named for the Revolutionary cause. McIntosh, Long, and Bryan were later carved from these early counties.

The Revolution created a virtual state of civil war in Georgia between loyalists and patriots. Along the coast, the older generation generally sympathized with the mother country, while their children espoused the cause of Liberty. In 1777, the loyalists were briefly expelled from Georgia. In 1778, a slave named Quanimo Dolly, known as Quash, revealed to the British fleet Walls Cut, a manmade passage through the marshes surrounding the Savannah River, which enabled the British to slip past the American lines, recapture Savannah, and restore royal government.

With the help of French, Polish, and Black troops from the French West Indies, the Americans hoped to rout the British from Savannah once again. On the morning of October 9, 1779, they attacked the waiting British forces at the Spring Hill Redoubt west of Savannah. The assault was repulsed after the allied troops sustained 752 men killed or wounded. British casualties were only fifty-seven. With this bloody defeat, British rule continued in Savannah until July 1782. Sunbury and the Salzburger town of Ebenezer fell to the British in January 1779, and, like Savannah, Ebenezer was occupied until 1782—a rare instance of two colonial cities under royal government throughout the Revolution.

The Revolution in Georgia produced its share of patriotic leaders and romantic heroes. Lyman Hall went on to become a governor of Georgia. A monument was erected in Savannah to commemorate the brave Polish count Casimir Pulaski, who died from wounds received at the Siege of Savannah. Another monument in Savannah recalls the well-publicized story that Sgt. Jasper was mortally wounded retrieving the colors of his regiment. Some heroes are known only through the veil of tradition, like Robert Sallette, a legendary guerrilla fighter who bloodied the loyalists in Liberty County.

Naturalists and Botanical Gardens

Following the Revolution, botanical explorers roamed the horti-culturally rich coastal region establishing collection gardens and branch nurseries on coastal plantations. In 1786, Andre Michaux, a French botanist, established gardens near Charleston, South Carolina, as an assembly point for the plants he collected. Michaux was instrumental in importing such foreign plants to southern gardens as the chinaberry tree and the common crape myrtle.

A similar garden was maintained by John Lyon on the plantation of Phineas Miller on Cumberland Island. Thomas Jefferson knew of many of these gardens. He was particularly interested in the botanical ability of John Couper of St. Simons Island and sent olive trees to the experimental gardens Couper maintained on his plantation at Cannon's Point.

The fertile river swamps of the Ogeechee, Newports, and Altamaha rivers drew naturalists and collectors from all over the world. Many of them traveled along the Fort Barrington Road, an old post road used by William Bartram in 1765 and 1773. In the accounts of his trip, Bartram noted the many rice plantations being carved from the swamps. He and his son John discovered the rare white flowered Franklinia and were among the last people to see it in bloom in the wild. Fortunately for posterity, the Bartrams carried specimens of this beautiful tree to their gardens in Philadelphia for propagation.

The native plants that so intrigued these collectors included the magnolia grandiflora, live oak, yellow jessamine, flowering dogwood, Hymenocallis, and wild azaleas. The planters also recognized the possibility of cultivating and improving native species. Thomas Fuller Hazzard, owner of West Point plantation on St. Simons Island, wrote extensively about propagating the fringe tree, pink and crimson swamp honeysuckle, and the numerous lilies that grew along the shady river banks.

This contact with foreign collectors also introduced many new species into cultivation in the South. Some of the most familiar plants associated with this region today are not native. Camellia japonica was brought to this country between 1798 and 1800, and by 1814 was in cultivation in Liberty County. Most of the evergreen azaleas that bloom so profusely in our modern gardens are natives of the Orient. The Cherokee rose, the state flower of Georgia, was possibly brought to the South by the Spanish. Even the prolific Chinese star (Confederate) jasmine was an antebellum import from the Far East.

Louis LeConte laid out an internationally recognized bulb and camellia garden within sight of his extensive inland rice fields at Woodmanston Plantation on Bulltown Swamp in Liberty County. His collections of native species provided many new specimens for English gardens.

The Post-Revolutionary Coastal Frontier

Much of the rice produced in the Midway region prior to the turn of the eighteenth century was shipped through the port of Sunbury. At the time Woodmanston was being assembled, Sunbury rivaled Savannah in port activity. One can only speculate, however, why Sunbury failed to reestablish into prominence after the Revolution. Perhaps it was because it had been burned by the British during the Revolution; or perhaps its unprotected proximity to the coast made it particularly vulnerable to hurricanes. Also, cotton began to supplant rice as a bulk commodity, and the large brokerage houses were in Savannah. Two ports so close together were simply not practical, and the smaller one probably was gradually supplanted by the larger port.

Oglethope's first land cessions from the Creeks, obtained soon after he arrived, opened the colony for settlement to the Altamaha. Even in the late nineteenth century when rafts of lumber were brought down the river, the raft men referred to the left and right banks as "White" and "Indian." Further cessions in 1763 extended the border to the St. Marys River. After 1763, there was a relentless push westward into Indian territory.

Although the frontier was receding in the 1780s and 1790s, sporadic raids by Indians made rural life on coastal plantations hazardous. In 1789, a party of Creeks attacked Woodmanston. The Savannah newspaper recounted the story.

> "On Wednesday morning, as soon as Dr. LeConte's Negroes had turned out of the Fort, the Indians attempted to seize on them. Six fellows went out with guns; as soon as the Negroes discovered the Indians they made back for the fort, and the Indians pursued them; there were some Negroes in the fort with arms, who, with the Doctor, fired on them, whilst those who went out armed attacked them in the rear, which soon made them retreat with some loss to a fence."

Joseph LeConte, the grandson of Dr. John Eatton LeConte, refers to this incident in his *Autobiography* stating that Dr. LeConte, anticipating an attack, had built a stockade and fortified it with Revolutionary muskets that they fired through loopholes. This was not the only house on the coast to have accommodations for defense. The tabby house at Wormsloe, ca. 1739, was also fortified, and a house on Edisto Island in South Carolina built in the late eighteenth century also had slits in the walls through which attackers could be fired on. In the Woodmanston raid, five slaves were captured by the Indians. Two escaped and returned to the plantation a few years after the attack. One slave, called Tomban, returned to the plantation in 1820, more than thirty years after he was abducted.

The Cotton Economy

The frontier seemed far away, however, when George Washington made his triumphal national tour. A thunderous welcome greeted General Washington's arrival in Savannah in 1791. Shortly after his departure, Washington sent two six-pounder bronze field pieces from the battlefield of Yorktown to the Chatham Artillery Company. On Washington's death, cities around the state, including St. Marys, planted oaks to commemorate this venerated first president of the United States.

Much of the town that Washington saw was devastated by a raging fire in 1796. By 1799, however, the city had expanded to twelve squares and on the ashes of wooden structures rose elegant brick dwellings, such as the Oliver Sturges House, signaling an era of new prosperity. The basis of this prosperity lay in the growing and shipping of cotton, an industry invigorated by Eli Whitney's perfection of the cotton gin while a guest at Mulberry Grove near Savannah in 1793.

Fortunes were made in the cotton trade and the merchants erected splendid edifices. The commission for the Independent Presbyterian Church was awarded as the result of a competition to John Holden Green, an architect from Rhode Island. Simultaneously, a series of mansions were being built by the young English architect William Jay. In 1819, the Independent Presbyterian Church was dedicated. The service was attended by President James Monroe who was in town for the launching of the transatlantic voyage of the Steamship Savannah. He was entertained in a house designed by Jay for William Scarbrough. In 1825, the Marquis de Lafayette greeted the citizens of Savannah from the beautiful regency style house commissioned by Richard Richardson in 1816. While in Savannah, Lafayette laid the cornerstone for the Nathanael Greene monument.

On the southern edge of the state, the Port of St. Marys, founded in 1787, also began to flourish. In less than forty years, the influence of cotton and shipping had enabled residents to construct fine Greek revival mansions such as Orange Hall, whose wide columned portico stands as a proud reminder of those days of prosperity and expansion. "King Cotton" reigned throughout the South, but its impact was nowhere more visibly concentrated than in the southern ports.

Cotton is mentioned in the *Colonial Records of Georgia* as a crop as early as 1740. A *Treatise on the State of the Province* prepared by Noble Jones and others described the trouble planters were having at the time cleansing the seed from the cotton. The cotton gin radically changed the course of the southern economy by solving this problem. Also about 1786, the seed of a long staple cotton of fine fiber was introduced into cultivation along the coast of Georgia. James Spalding of St. Simons Island was one of the first planters to plant the seed that came to be known as Sea Island cotton and generated a worldwide demand.

Cultivation of the crop demanded extensive clearing of fields. Large landholdings were amassed and a plantation system developed. St. Simons Island alone had more than a dozen plantations including Cannon's Point, Hamilton, Hampton, and Retreat. Prior to the building of the railroads, access to waterways for transportation was essential, therefore the plantations were often positioned on bluffs overlooking these river highways. Frequently their names reflected this situation. Gascoigne Bluff, Butlers Point, and Black Banks were all on St. Simons.

A statistical table compiled by Alexander Wylly of St. Simons Island for the years 1820 through 1823 gives an idea of the extent of cultivation and clearing of land that occurred along the coast before the Civil War. Seventeen planters were listed in the table with 1,668 acres of land cleared and planted in cotton on St. Simons. By 1860, 19,000 acres had been cleared for cultivation. The total yield in Georgia had grown from 1,000 bales of upland and Sea Island cotton at the beginning of the cotton era to more than 701,000 bales by 1860.

Rice continued to be an important commodity along the Georgia coast in the antebellum period. The eighteenth-century inland swamp, or gravity flow system, was replaced by the tidal flow system, which used the natural ebb and flow of the tides for irrigation. Hofwyl Plantation in Glynn County retains evidence of the dams and canals that were successfully used for five generations of rice cultivation.

A handful of planters experimented with growing sugar cane in the early nineteenth century. About 1806, Thomas Spalding acquired seeds from John Couper and made a planting on Sapelo. Having developed a successful method for growing the crop, he constructed a tabby sugar mill about 1812. Other tabby sugar mills, such as the New Canaan Plantation sugar mill near St. Marys and the Thicket in McIntosh County, were also constructed.

Cane sugar production continued in Georgia on a small scale throughout the nineteenth century. On the farms, syrup making was a social occasion and Georgia cane syrup is still considered a fine topping for breakfast biscuits. Today, sugars—beet and corn—are refined in a large plant on the Savannah River and refined sugar composes one of the principal exports through that port.

Plantation Life

The production of cotton, rice, and sugar cane required an enormous amount of hand labor. In 1753, shortly after the restrictions against slavery in Georgia had been lifted, the Black population of the colony was only 1,066. By 1790, this figure had risen to 52,886 and Blacks accounted for nearly seventy percent of the total population of the rice coast.

In 1798, the direct importation of African slaves was prohibited in Georgia, and direct slave trading with Africa was made a federal offense in 1808. But just as pirate ships were able to use the coastal maze of waterways to elude detection by the Crown, so did the illegal African slave ships slip in and out among the many tributaries without fear of discovery. Slave smuggling existed as late as 1858 when the slave ship Wanderer made its last Georgia run. The desire on the part of many slaves to return to Africa was strong, at times bringing tragic results. Such is the story of Ebo Landing on St. Simons where legend tells of a group of shackled slaves who chose to drown by marching into the river rather than be subjected to slavery.

Not all Blacks were slaves in Georgia. Many free persons of color, such as Simon Mirault in Savannah, came from the French West Indies. They were educated and owned property. Others bought their freedom, as did the Reverend Andrew Bryan in 1790. While a slave he organized the first Black Baptist church in America in 1788 in a barn on Brampton Plantation. His portrait may be seen in the handsome stained glass windows of the First African Baptist Church in Savannah.

The coastal Blacks of the nineteenth century contributed much to the historic legacy of the region. Bessie Jones, a folk singer on St. Simons has devoted her life to collecting the Black game and work songs that she and the Sea Island Singers continue to perpetuate.

The houses for the slaves were small, built in parallel rows facing one another to form a wide street. Thomas Spalding revived the practice of making tabby about 1810 when he employed it in the construction of his home on Sapelo Island. Spalding published his methods for the benefit of other planters, and in the next few decades many coastal structures, including slave cabins, were built of this durable material. Some of these early nineteenth century dwellings may still be seen on St. Simons, Cumberland, Sapelo, and St. Catherines islands.

The typical plantation settlement consisted of a main house, overseer's house, slave cabins, kitchen and service buildings, agricultural structures and, on larger plantations, a hospital such as the one whose ruins remain at Retreat on St. Simons Island. These structures were built in direct response to the climate and were constructed of locally available material, primarily wood and tabby. They were simple cottages pleasantly situated among groves of live oaks, cedars, and magnolias. Most were raised one story out of reach of flood waters brought by hurricanes. These powerful storms with winds over one hundred miles per hour have on several occasions driven water over the coastal islands. Only by elevating structures could flooding be avoided.

Frances Butler Leigh, daughter of Pierce Butler, describes the house at Hampton: "There were four good-sized rooms down and two upstairs, with a hall ten feet wide running through the house and a wide verandah shut in from the sun by venetian shades running around it; the kitchen with servant's quarters, was as usual detatched."

Alleys of oaks were planted to shade the avenues that led to the houses and slave quarters. A magnificent double alley remains at Retreat (Sea Island Golf Club) on St. Simons, and a more recent alley set out in the 1890s may be seen at Wormsloe in Chatham County.

Plantation owners occupied their plantations on a seasonal basis. In the summer, the dangers of fever, particularly on the rice plantations, forced the owners to seek cooler, dryer locations. Although fever had long been associated with wet locations, it was not until the 1890s that the disease was recognized to be carried by mosquitoes that bred in areas of standing water.

To escape the unhealthy fevers the planters built summer homes on the mainland in pine forests on elevated sand ridges or located them on salt water. Walthourville and Flemington in Liberty County are two sand ridge towns that began as summer retreats. These retreats attracted so many families that missions of the Midway Church were established to facilitate summer worship. The oldest, Flemington Presbyterian Church, was organized about 1815. The present church was built in 1852 and still has an active congregation. The Walthourville Church was organized before 1855, and the present structure was built in 1884. The Dorchester Community began attracting residents about 1843. Descendants of the families who lived there return each fall for a special service in the Dorchester Church, ca. 1854.

Baisden's Bluff, now known as Crescent, in McIntosh County was an early nineteenth-century summer retreat with a salt water location. The D'Antignac House at Crescent is one of the oldest summer cottages in the area and dates from ca. 1790. One story associated with this house is that it was the home of the Reverend Francis Robert Goulding, author in 1825 of the children's classic *Young Marooners*.

The owners of these coastal plantations were aristocratic men of letters who played important roles in political and cultural endeavors. James Hamilton Couper, owner of Hopeton and Altama on the mainland in Glynn County and Cannon's Point on St. Simons, was outstanding among Georgia planters of the day. He conducted his planting operations on the basis of scientific research and experimentation and was a pioneer in the crushing of cotton seed for oil. Also an amateur architect, he designed Christ Church at Savannah and his houses at Hopeton and Altama.

Aaron Burr, vice president of the United States, spent the summer and fall of 1804 at Hampton on Butler's Point after the duel in which he killed Alexander Hamilton. During his trip, he also visited Savannah and St. Marys. Fanny Kemble, a famous English actress and ardent abolitionist, was married to Major Pierce Butler. Her journal of the daily events at Butler's Point and the rice plantation near Darien was published as *A Journal of a Residence on a Georgian Plantation, 1838-1839*. Coastal Georgia was surprisingly cosmopolitan.

Port Prosperity

In addition to the Sea Island variety grown along the coast, cotton was also concentrated in the piedmont area of Georgia. The Savannah River was navigable to Augusta, so when Georgians built a rail line from Augusta to the interior, Savannah became the trading center for cotton producers throughout the state. Enterprising South Carolinians, however, built a rail line from Charleston to Hamburg, just across the river from Augusta, and threatened to siphon off this trade. The construction of the Central of Georgia Railroad from Savannah to the piedmont averted this danger and contributed greatly to the subsequent success of the Port of Savannah.

In 1859, Savannah was the factoring center for the cotton and rice planters. Here the planters came to conduct their business and to socialize with their neighbors. The factors' offices were located in the five-story ranges that lined the river bluff for one mile. A factor was an essential member of the southern economy, serving the planter in many ways—lending money for seeds and fertilizer, selling the crop, and ordering personal goods for the planter and his family.

Day and night one could hear the rumble of the wheels of the drays over the brick streets transporting the cotton to the waiting steamers on the river. The cotton trade precipitated a building boom along the coast. In the 1850s, speculating developers built row after row of Savannah grey brick, high-stoop townhouses. Wealthy planters and merchants hired notable architects like John Norris of New York and Irish-born Charles Cluskey, who worked to erect mansions like the gothic revival Green-Meldrim House and the Greek revival Champion-McAlpin-Fowlkes House. Foundries forged cast iron balconies that stand out in stark relief against the soft stucco facades of the houses. Plantation cotton fed the prosperity of Savannah, and the resulting trade brought considerable contact with and influence from northern cities and Europe, especially England.

Cotton was everywhere, lining the streets from the freight warehouses of the new Central of Georgia Railroad depot on West Broad Street all the way to the bay. Of this new complex Colburn's *New York Railroad Advocate* wrote in 1855, "We doubt candidly, if any other station can be found in the country which can equal this."

The War Between the States

The agrarian economy of Georgia and its dependence on slavery, like that of the rest of the southern states, created an entirely different culture than that evolving in the industrial North. Lincoln's election in November 1860 threatened to topple this slave-based economy and precipitated a conflict that had been fomenting for more than a decade.

The news of the secession of South Carolina in December 1860 was celebrated in coastal Georgia. A flag was raised in Johnson Square in Savannah, and it pictured a rattlesnake with the inscription "Don't Tread on Me." There was a torchlight procession and illumination in support of South Carolina. Many believed that there would not be a war but, if it came, a rapid victory was predicted for the Confederacy. When the commander of the federal forces stationed in Charleston harbor secretly moved his small garrison to Fort Sumter in the middle of the harbor, however, the slave-holding states were enraged and frightened.

Georgians met to discuss what course of action to take, and in January 1861, Georgia became the fifth state to secede from the Union. Georgia Governor Joseph E. Brown ordered Colonel Alexander R. Lawton to assemble a group of men from the Savannah Volunteer Guards, the Oglethorpe Light Infantry, and the Chatham Artillery to seize Fort Pulaski, a federal fortification located at the mouth of the Savannah River. With only a caretaker in residence, the soldiers encountered no resistance and easily claimed the unmanned fort. Fort Pulaski had been built as a part of a network of coastal fortifications begun by President Monroe after the War of 1812. Although Cockspur Island was chosen as the site of a fort in 1812, it was not until 1829 that construction was actually underway. That year, an engineer, young Robert E. Lee, came to Cockspur for his first military assignment—to begin the system of drainage and dikes for the island. The massive solid brick fort was far too heavy to be supported on the mucky soil of the island, and today it still literally floats on the mud on massive timber pilings.

Many problems delayed the construction of the fort, so that by 1860 only twenty guns out of an armament of 146 were in place and no garrison had been assigned. It was in this unfinished condition that the militia seized the fort for the State of Georgia. Slaves and state militiamen worked furiously to ready the fort for action. Additional guns were secured, and a telegraph line was erected to Savannah. Fort Jackson, five miles from Savannah on the Savannah River, was also placed in order. This masonry fort had been rebuilt in 1842 on the site of an old colonial battery to protect the inner harbor.

On April 12, 1861, at 4:30 a.m. Confederate batteries around Charleston Harbor opened fire on Fort Sumter, forcing the federal garrison to depart. Civil war enveloped the nation.

Georgia was not prepared for a sustained military engagement. Its economic resources were tied up in cotton and slaves. There was no industrial base to speak of. The "navy" of Georgia consisted of a "mosquito" fleet of rebuilt paddle wheelers and tugboats that were no match for superior federal naval forces. Federal strategy was to blockade the coast immediately and bottle up the principal navigation routes. In the fall of 1861, the Union navy took Hilton Head and Port Royal in South Carolina within sight of Tybee Island. When a naval blockade was set up outside the entrance of the Savannah River, Georgia reacted by abandoning the coastal islands, feeling that it would take too many men to adequately protect the beaches. An inner line of defense was secured, which, in addition to Forts Pulaski and Jackson, included Fort McAllister, an earthwork fort at the mouth of the Ogeechee River, and a series of batteries. Fort Pulaski, the state of the art in military fortification, was considered impregnable from land and naval bombardment.

Working secretly at night, Union forces set up a remarkable series of batteries on Tybee Island opposite Fort Pulaski, camouflaging their work by day. These batteries were armed with the new rifled cannons that were off-loaded on the opposite side of the island and dragged across the sand and marshes to the gun emplacements. Captain Quincy A. Gillmore of the Union forces believed the new guns to be accurate enough for repeated bombardment of a target and therefore capable of penetrating the thick masonry walls of Fort Pulaski. He risked his career to prove his point.

The bombardment began on April 10, 1862. After thirty hours a breach was achieved. Soon projectiles were threatening the powder magazine on the opposite side of the parade ground of the fort, and little could be done but surrender. The accuracy and penetrating power of the rifled cannon had been proven, marking the end of an age of military thinking and fortifications.

As federal troops occupied the islands, Georgia plantation owners abandoned their cotton plantations and moved their slaves inland. The Confederates determined that the islands were indefensible, but before abandoning them they destroyed certain strategic buildings like the lighthouse on St. Simons and the original Oglethorpe Hotel in Brunswick.

The effects of the blockade were felt in a lack of consumer goods, but food was plentiful. With the exception of Darien, which was burned by the federals in the summer of 1863, the coast saw little action through most of the war. General William T. Sherman brought the battle to the coast late in the war, cutting a bitter swath through the heart of the cotton belt in Georgia. His goal was to sever the rail lines and confiscate all useful commodities. In December 1864, he reached Fort McAllister, which, having withstood several naval attacks during the war, fell to Sherman's army in fierce hand-to-hand combat. Sherman watched the engagement from a nearby rice mill and then proceeded to Savannah.

Seeing that it would be impossible to hold Savannah any longer, Confederate troops evacuated the city by creating a pontoon bridge of rice barges across the channels of the Savannah River. By the glow of burning and scuttled ships in the harbor, hundreds of troops were safely evacuated from the city. When Sherman finally entered the city on December 21, 1864, the city was virtually abandoned. Sherman was offered quarters in the gothic revival mansion of English-born merchant Charles Green. From Savannah Sherman sent his well-known telegram to President Lincoln, "I beg to present you as a Christmas gift the City of Savannah, with one hundred and fifty guns and plenty of ammunition, also about twenty-five thousand bales of cotton."

Sherman's march across Georgia left a devastating trail. Encountering little resistance on plantations occupied only by women, children, and slaves, the troops confiscated the abundant food resources and often destroyed what they could not use. During Sherman's one month occupation of the area, his men repeatedly invaded coastal plantations, arbitrarily violating the sanctity of defenseless homes, carrying off or killing the livestock, and threatening the Blacks who would not leave.

In Savannah, the Stars and Stripes were suspended across a street so that the Savannah women would have to walk under it. One lady refused and a squad of soldiers compelled her to march back and forth under it several times. Some of the churches were closed, and a seal was put on the doors of Christ Church because the ministers refused to pray for the president of the United States. Once a week the inhabitants of Savannah received their rations: grist, a piece of bacon, some Yankee beans, and a pound or so of pilot bread. Conditions were hard, however, Savannah was spared the fiery fates of Atlanta and Columbia.

Reconstruction—the Economy Changes

Although the coast saw little of the action that enveloped other areas of the South, Georgia had placed 125,000 men in battle, 25,000 of whom were killed. Georgia faced Reconstruction with few able-bodied men and little capital.

The planters who returned to the coast after the Civil War found their plantations, railroads, and economy in ruins. Many families who were not able to return to their farms migrated to urban centers like Savannah and Brunswick. Brunswick grew rapidly from a population of two thousand in 1880 to twelve thousand by 1900. This influx of people prompted an immediate need for housing and attention to improved transportation. The Victorian District in Savannah developed during this period and was a direct result of the establishment of a streetcar system in 1869. Building and loan associations enabled families of modest means to build frame houses with plans and details ordered from catalogs and payments on a monthly basis.

Although cotton production once again began to dominate Georgia agriculture, without slave labor it was a more expensive crop to grow. Wages had to be paid and more and more fertilizer bought to replenish a depleted soil. It became harder to compete with the prices and productivity of the more fertile cotton lands of west Georgia and Alabama. Cotton trading continued to be brisk on the floors of the ornate Cotton Exchange in Savannah for a few decades, but, by the second decade of the twentieth century, cotton had ceased entirely to be a profit-making crop in Georgia. Rice production also ceased about this time. A devastating series of storms flooded the fields with salt water and rendered them temporarily useless. At the same time more efficient dry culture methods began to be employed in such states as Arkansas and Texas.

Georgians turned to other crops and commodities to rebuild their economy. Pecan production and tobacco replaced cotton, but the most important element in the new economy had been growing for centuries in the abundant forests of coastal Georgia. Sawmills were built in Darien, St. Marys, on St. Simons, and elsewhere to tap the vast timber resources. The cut timber was floated down the rivers from the inland swamps and forests tied together in huge rafts. The strong and durable wood of the live oaks at Gascoigne Bluff on St. Simons was used in the construction of the renowned eighteenth-century warship, the U. S. S. Constitution (Old Ironsides), and later, in the nineteenth century, timbers for the Brooklyn Bridge were sawed in a mill at that same bluff. The harvesting of swamp cypress, meanwhile, was a dangerous and back-breaking job, but it was done so thoroughly that the only stand of virgin cypress left in coastal Georgia is in the middle of tiny Lewis Island, deep in the Altamaha basin.

Darien, Brunswick, Savannah, and St. Marys became great timber ports in the late nineteenth century. In 1885, the port of Darien had five foreign consuls, three sawmills, and loaded ninety-five million board feet of lumber onto vessels from many countries. Within ten years Brunswick would surpass this feat.

Some of the mills were built on old plantation sites. The Dodge-Meigs mill was constructed on the site of Hamilton Plantation on St. Simons and employed as many as one thousand people. Churches were built on mill property for the workers, including the Victorian-style Union Church, now called Lovely Lane Chapel.

Lighthouses destroyed during the Civil War were rebuilt to guide the ships into the harbors. The Tybee Lighthouse, standing 145 feet high, was completed in 1867. The beacon from its fresnel lens is visible for eighteen miles. The St. Simons Lighthouse and Keeper's Cottage date from 1872 and were one of the last works of the architect Charles B. Cluskey. Antebellum blind lights exist on Cockspur Island and the north end of Little Cumberland Island.

Reconstruction—Freedom for Blacks

For the freed slaves, predominantly raised without any formal education, there was the enormous task of coping with emancipation—which gave them their freedom on paper, but, in reality, little else. General Sherman issued Special Field Order #15, which promised the freedmen forty-acre homesteads on the islands and abandoned rice fields along the coast, but, without capital to pay taxes and equipment to cultivate the land, the grants gradually reverted to white ownership.

For a brief time, coastal Georgia was home to a Black separatist nation with its capital on St. Catherines Island. Tunis Campbell of Massachusetts had come to Georgia as an agent for the Freedmen's Bureau. In time, however, he established an autocratic government and ruled with a firm hand until he was removed forcibly to Darien by federal agents in 1866. Later he was one of the first Blacks to be elected to the Georgia Senate.

Some Blacks gathered in communities such as Harrington and Jew Town on St. Simons or Jerusalem near St. Marys and found work in the lumber mills. Others simply returned to their former plantations and took up subsistence farming and sharecropping.

Like their former owners, many Blacks also migrated to the urban centers. A neighborhood grew up on the east side of Savannah and a school, the Beach Institute, was established in 1867 for the education of Black children. Blacks took jobs as carpenters, coopers, bricklayers, butchers, porters, and pattern makers.

Immediately following the Civil War, support for the development of Black educational institutions came from northern church and missionary societies such as the American Missionary Society, which had founded the Beach Institute. Another missionary school of note along the Georgia coast was the Dorchester Academy in Liberty County. For most rural Black children, however, their only education for many years was in primary level one-room schoolhouses that they attended sporadically between tending crops.

The first state-sponsored public institution of higher education for Blacks was organized in 1890. The Georgia State Industrial College for Colored Youths, now known as Savannah State College, is located in Thunderbolt, near Savannah.

Independent Black religious congregations were organized during Reconstruction in great numbers in urban and rural areas. The American Missionary Society formed the First Congregational Church in 1867, and its present handsome gothic revival building was constructed in 1895. Contributions toward the construction of St. Cyprians Episcopal Church in Darien came from England and Philadelphia through the philanthropy of Pierce Butler's daughter, Frances, and her husband, the Reverend James Wentworth Leigh. This unusual tabby church still stands on a bluff in Darien.

Transportation Improvements and the Resort Era

One of the primary goals of Sherman's march had been to destroy the railroad systems. Rails were pulled and bent around trees to ensure their destruction—"Sherman's neckties" dotted the landscape. Therefore, an important early post-war task was to repair the damaged lines and to replenish the rolling stock, while adding new roads to the system. These lines connected the coast with the timber producing interior. New towns, such as Willie and Allenhurst in Liberty County and Cox and Townsend in McIntosh County, all owe their origin to the expansion of the railroads. Older communities, like Guyton in Effingham County, laid out in 1838, became summer retreats for Savannah businessmen as the railroads began to offer easy access to the city.

The railroads and streetcar lines also provided nineteenth-century Georgians access to recreational sites on the rivers and marshes. Isle of Hope and Thunderbolt in Chatham County were two of these destinations. A summer community called Ridgeville, or the Ridge, flourished near Darien. Here on a sandy ridge timber pilots and merchants built lovely two-story houses with wide ornate verandahs for the enjoyment of refreshing marsh breezes.

For the poet Sidney Lanier, the peaceful solitude of the oaks and marshes surrounding Brunswick inspired him to write in 1875 one of his greatest poems, *The Marshes of Glynn*. In fact, the scenic beauty of coastal Georgia began to attract many people, who, although less capable of literary expression, were just as moved by its wonder. Greater leisure time, the democratizing of disposable income, and the increased accessibility of some of the coastal islands signaled the beginning of the tourist era.

The majority of the islands along the coast after the Civil War quickly reverted to their natural state. A few like Sapelo became the private hunting retreats of northern financiers and industrialists. The most renowned of these was the exclusive Jekyll Island Club established in 1886. It was frequented in the winter months by some of the most significant families of American industrial wealth—the Vanderbilts, Rockefellers, Astors, and Goulds—who established a golf course and indoor tennis courts for their sole enjoyment. They built grand "cottages" and an apartment house. In keeping with the vacation spirit, the cottages were not equipped with kitchens and meals were taken at the main clubhouse.

Dungeness on Cumberland Island had been the property of Revolutionary War hero General Nathanael Greene. After Greene's death, his widow moved with her new husband, Phineas Miller, to Cumberland where they maintained the house and its magnificent walled gardens. Here, in 1818, Light Horse Harry Lee died, and, although his body was later reinterred at Washington and Lee in Virginia, a marker in the Dungeness graveyard commemorates the memory of the father of Robert E. Lee. In the late-nineteenth century, Cumberland was purchased by the Carnegie and Candler families who created elegant enclaves on the island. The Candlers built on the north end while the Carnegies constructed a new Dungeneess on the south end, as well as several other notable houses including Plum Orchard and Greyfield, now an inn.

For the not so wealthy, picnic excursions by steamer were made to the beaches of Tybee Island and St. Simons. In 1887, a train link was completed from Savannah to Tybee, confirming its popularity as an ocean resort destination. A trip aboard the train was not without its occasional inconvenience, however, for often the tracks would spread apart on the soft mud, leaving the train stranded on the marsh flats. The passengers would then have to walk the track back to Savannah or Tybee, whichever was closer.

Until the 1920s, St. Simons was only accessible by ferryboat. Despite this inconvenience, seaside hotels flourished. The typical hotel of the 1880s was a rambling wooden structure with adjacent cottages for family accommodations. On St. Simons and Cumberland islands, horse and mule-drawn trolleys on rails met the steamers and transported the guests to the hotels. On the mainland, large resort hotels, such as the Oglethorpe (now demolished) in Brunswick, were built for the tourists attracted by the mild winter season in coastal Georgia.

Designed by the New York architect J. A. Wood, who designed many hotels along the new railroads in Florida and Georgia, the Oglethorpe was co-owned with the Hotel St. Simons. In the summer, the Oglethorpe would be closed and all the interior furnishings moved over to the island—this action was then reversed at the close of the summer season.

Some families preferred to build their own summer cottages. Built without electricity or other conveniences, their names reflect a tranquil seasonal use—Take-It-Easy, Bluebird, and Tillandsia (the scientific name for Spanish moss, a graceful epiphytic member of the pineapple family).

A Brunswick newspaper remarked after the turn of the century that "the type of folk who can afford a seaside vacation usually own a car and want to use it on their trip." Those who did arrive in the coastal region by car drove from Savannah to Darien over the same route surveyed by Oglethorpe in Colonial times. At Darien, the automobiles were loaded onto the flat cars of the Georgia Coast and Piedmont Railroad, affectionately known as the "Get Out, Cuss, and Push" or the "Gator, Coon, and Possum Road," and they were transported across the marshy expanse of the Altamaha delta to Brunswick and points south.

This shortline railroad that connected Jacksonville with Ludowici through Brunswick and Darien was vital to the growth of Brunswick and the Golden Isles as a "charming winter resort." An increasingly bountiful flow of northern visitors flocked to enjoy the coastal climate, which John Wesley had described in 1736 as "the bloom of spring in the depth of winter." More hotels were built, like the Riverview in St. Marys, to receive the onslaught of tourists.

The Automobile and the Twentieth Century

With the demise of the GP&C Railroad in the 1920s, several men worked concurrently to bring a paved coastal highway into being. Harvey Granger, a real estate developer and automotive pioneer in Savannah, was a principal backer of the coastal highway link that was proposed to cross what at the time were considered impassable marshes and swamps. Granger had also been responsible for a paved causeway from the mainland to Tybee paralleling the old rail bed.

Another promoter of the paved highway was Howard Coffin, co-founder and chief engineer of the Hudson Motor Company. In 1911, he purchased Sapelo Island and later also purchased Long Island, a small wild island off St. Simons which he renamed Sea Island.

Coffin envisioned a carefully planned family resort community that would draw a national tourist market. He wanted to build a resort hotel on Sea Island which would be the only one between Pinehurst in North Carolina and Daytona Beach in Florida. A causeway to St. Simons was completed in 1924 and was a key element in the success of his venture. Coffin had to undertake many physical and transportation improvements, which incidentally also improved the quality of life for Brunswick and the communities on St. Simons. He arranged for southbound trains to stop near Brunswick to discharge passengers for Sea Island and also made accommodations for the Ocean Steamship Company to bring package tours to Savannah from Boston and New York. The tourists were then bussed to Sea Island by his Coastal Transport Company, which he later sold to the Greyhound Bus Company. Coffin was also responsible for helping to establish an airport on St. Simons.

At the south end of Sea Island, the Spanish-style Cloister Hotel was constructed. Its architect, Addison Mizner, had designed many Palm Beach estates. Attractive cottages began to line the meticulously manicured lanes. Visiting notables from around the world, such as playwright Eugene O'Neill, established an atmosphere of refined seclusion.

It is not surprising with the Scottish influence along the coast that golf was played here as early as 1795—Savannah at that time had an active golf club. One of the first golf courses in the South was laid out on Jekyll Island in 1894, and the Savannah Golf Club course was built in 1899. The Scottish game was ideal for the mild coastal climate, and soon enthusiasts were flocking to the courses.

In 1927, Coffin built a beautiful golf course on St. Simons at Retreat Plantation. Designed by Walter Travis and later redesigned by the English firm of Colt and Alison, the course meanders beneath centuries-old oaks over former cotton fields, passing by the tabby ruins of former plantation buildings. With this Plantation Nine and the construction of additional nines, the Sea Island Company has developed a golfing complex of international fame.

Using the Sea Island course as an inspiration and model and the coastal beauty as a natural amenity, other developers have built courses throughout the area, providing hundreds of holes of challenging golf.

The automobile not only brought tourists to the coast to play golf but was in part responsible for a new wave of suburban growth. About 1910, two planned subdivisions were conceived south of Victory Drive in Savannah. Ardsley Park and Chatham Crescent featured landscaped parks and squares surrounded by an eclectic mix of early twentieth century-revival styles.

Nowhere is the Spanish revival style more prevalent than in Ludowici in Long County. On its 137-mile journey to the sea, the Altamaha unloads its deposits of red and green middle Georgia clay in the deltas surrounding Ludowici. The contributions of the river to the economy of coastal Georgia have been numerous—from the irrigation of rice fields to the transport for lumber barges—but for Ludowici the Altamaha provided the clay for colorful roof tiles characteristic of the Spanish revival style. Between 1904 and 1914, the Ludowici Celadon tile factory transformed the clay deposits into brick and tile. Today twenty-eight tile roofed buildings and the site of the tile factory remain in Ludowici.

Another northern industrialist attracted to the Georgia coast in the early years of the twentieth century was Henry Ford. In 1925, he bought Richmond Hill Plantation in Bryan County and built a winter home on the Great Ogeechee River in 1936. The original home, rice mill, and slave quarters were burned by Sherman during the Civil War. Henry Ford engaged in social and humanitarian endeavors to improve the life of nearby residents, both Black and White. Seventy-five percent of the people near his farm were Black. For these people he built a grammar school and a high school, a machine shop, and set up night classes for the adults. He experimented with the industrial use of agricultural products and opened a sawmill. He developed a Ford farm house prototype on a production system which allowed the houses to be hauled anywhere in the South and put up by Ford carpenters complete for $2,500. His vocational-agricultural work progressed into the 1940s at Ford Farms. After his death in 1947, the experiment ended and the property passed into other hands.

Julius Rosenwald, president of Sears and Roebuck, left a part of his resources to better the condition of southern Blacks. Rosenwald allocated funds to construct schools for Blacks throughout the South. One such school was built in 1921 near St. Marys known as the Kinlaw Rosenwald School. It is now undergoing restoration by the Black community.

The Military Impact

The strategic position of Georgia in the defense of the Atlantic coast has led to a succession of military fortifications placed here by the British, the Colonials, the Confederacy, and the United States government. In 1897, several coastal defense batteries were constructed at Fort Screven on Tybee Island. This was the last artillery fortification to be built on the Georgia coast. By 1924, the original concrete gun emplacements and guns were considered to be obsolete targets for modern fast moving battleships and the coastal artillery companies were withdrawn.

In June 1940, air power was added to the coastal defense system. Fort Stewart, one of the largest military installations in land area in the United States, contains 300,000 acres and covers parts of five Georgia counties, including Liberty and Bryan. Entire communities were absorbed by the installation, including Taylor's Creek, one of the earliest settlements in Liberty County, Clyde, the former seat of Bryan County, Willie, and Letford. Fort Stewart was made a permanent army installation in 1956. Today the military plays an important role in the coastal economy with the continued presence of Hunter Army Airfield in Savannah and the development of Kings Bay Trident Nuclear Submarine Base in St. Marys.

Water Commerce

The ports of Savannah and Brunswick are still vital to the coastal economy. In 1896, the Savannah harbor, including parts of the main shipping channel, was still littered with the wrecks of scuttled ironclads and other ships destroyed during the Confederate evacuation of Savannah. That year a twenty-four foot channel was dredged and most of the obstructions removed, signaling the beginning of an effort to diversify the cargo passing through the port. Fertilizer, timber, refined sugar, cottonseed oil, cigars, and textiles began to replace the cotton and turpentine rosin (naval stores) that had dominated the economy of the port for so many years.

During World War II, eighty-eight liberty cargo ships were constructed in the port. In 1945, the Georgia Ports Authority was formed, and, since that time, the port, and its thirty-eight-foot-deep channel have grown to be the largest in international commerce on the south Atlantic. Among its largest exports are pulp, paper, and paperboard—produced by the pulp mills located in several coastal counties. The Brunswick port offers deepwater barge, railroad, and interstate highway access, making it an important bulk commodity port.

The fishing industry has also contributed significantly to the economy of the coast. Thunderbolt, Darien, and St. Marys are but a few of the old communities that harbor picturesque shrimping fleets. Shrimp, crab, oysters, and, when in season, Ogeechee shad are delicacies not to be missed.

Preservation in Coastal Georgia

The golden coast of Georgia is an enchanting, beautiful, civilized place with a vitality that is inspirational. The preservation of its environmental beauty and historic resources has been the cornerstone for the perpetuation and enjoyment of this very special part of America. Since the turn of the century, individuals, agencies, and organizations have spearheaded efforts to preserve historic sites along the coast. In general, these early efforts followed a national preservation movement that tended to memorialize important historic events, places, and individuals. In 1903, the Georgia Chapter of the National Society of Colonial Dames of America acquired a part of the Frederica tract in order to preserve the colonial fort ruins from further destruction. Later, the National Park Service designated it a national monument. Both organizations subsequently acquired other important sites—the Park Service designated Fort Pulaski a national monument in 1924, and the Colonial Dames restored the Andrew Low House in Savannah, the home of a wealthy nineteenth-century cotton merchant and father-in-law of Juliette Gordon Low, for use as their state headquarters.

The State of Georgia preserved several military fortifications along the coast, including Fort McAllister, Fort King George, and Fort Jackson. Fort Jackson is now privately administered.

In 1931, the Cassina Garden Club renovated two Hamilton Plantation slave cabins on St. Simons, and recently the Garden Club of Georgia has been hard at work on a plan to utilize the LeConte-Woodmanston Botanical Garden and Rice Plantation site in Liberty County. The Association for the Study of Afro-American Life and History maintains a Black history museum in Savannah in the renovated King-Tisdell Cottage. The Coastal Georgia Historical Society operates a museum in the St. Simons Lighthouse Keeper's Cottage, and the Salzburger Society keeps alive the memory of the exemplary settlers of Ebenezer.

In l955, the Historic Savannah Foundation was incorporated to preserve and protect the irreplaceable squares and architecture of that unique city. The foundation developed an aggressive approach to preservation, which became the focus of international attention, and commissioned a comprehensive architectural inventory of the 2.2-square-mile district comprising the original city plan. With the passage of the Historic Preservation Act of 1966, other communities also conducted surveys, and now architectural inventories are underway in all of the coastal counties. More than fifty buildings, sites, and districts are listed on the National Register of Historic Places in these counties, including thirteen historic districts containing nearly five thousand additional contributing structures. Recently, the efforts of the Savannah Landmark Rehabilitation Project have shown that people of all economic levels can and should be able to benefit from neighborhood revitalization.

As for the natural environment, landuse and ownership patterns have contributed to the preservation of the exhilarating native beauty of coastal Georgia. Wetlands and state and federal lands compose almost forty percent of the area. Another twenty-five percent is forested area maintained by pulp and paper companies. Thus, about sixty-five percent of the coastal region is relatively unavailable for development. The waterfront areas, however, are vulnerable to the overdevelopment problems that plague coastal lands throughout the country. To safeguard their splendor for the enjoyment of future generations, many Georgia islands have been transferred from private ownership to limited access public ownership. The establishment of design review districts for the remaining waterfront will assist planners and entrepreneurs in the further protection of the coastal landscape.

The result of these varied preservation efforts has not been the creation of a museum atmosphere of glass-encased artifacts and specimens, however, but rather the perpetuation of a living stage where the coastal environment, historic sites, and recreational activities naturally intertwine. The examples are everywhere—from the lush fairways winding through the forests and fields of Retreat Plantation to the nineteenth-century lighthouses that watch over sailboats, sunbathers, and fishermen, from cyclists rounding the squares of old Savannah to camping enthusiasts riding the ferry from St. Marys to Cumberland. The real treasure is not the pirate gold buried by Blackbeard—it is all about us—on the golden coast of Georgia.

7. OSSABAW SOUND

8. BEACH, OSSABAW ISLAND

9. OAK FOREST

The life of Georgia's vast new coastal plain varied greatly with the cold of glacial advance and the warmth of glacial retreat. In cold periods spruce forests grew as far south as Louisiana, and walrus hunted the waters off the Georgia coast. In the hot periods the plain was something like the present savanna of Africa. Shaggy, four-tusked mastodons wandered there, and true elephants larger than any of Africa's. There were lions, saber-toothed cats, cougars, bobcats, rhinoceroses, giant armadillo-like glyptodons, beavers as big as bears, camels, llamas, tapirs, peccaries, deer, dire wolves, horses, and several species of bison. There was megatherium, a ground sloth eighteen feet long. Its bones were massive—the femur was three times as thick as an elephant's—and the sloth must have weighed several tons. It was a slow-moving vegetarian of enormous strength. There was entelodont, a gigantic, nearly brainless pig that stood six feet at the shoulder. Great companies of these creatures wandered between the edge of the sea and the inland forests of magnolia, tupelo, sweetgum, tulip poplar, cypress, and other subtropical trees.

The life of the present beach gives a fair idea of what life was like on the five Pleistocene coastlines from which it has descended, as well as of the life on the seven Cretaceous and Tertiary coastlines behind them. The paper-thin horseshoe crab, essentially unchanged for 350 million years and not really a crab at all—its nearest kin are the spider and scorpion—still lives here.

Even the birdlife of this coast is ancient. The shorebirds: loons, grebes, petrels, pelicans, cormorants, anhingas, herons, egrets, bitterns, plovers, and curlews, are the most primitive of avians. Not only do they resemble reptiles in flight—the snake-necked water turkey, for example, as it feeds and flies in the marsh—but they also contain much kindred bone structure.

Robert Hanie,
GUALE, THE GOLDEN COAST OF GEORGIA

10. HORSESHOE CRAB

12. BROWN PELICAN

11. GREAT BLUE HERON

13. SPANISH MOSS

14. ANHINGA

15. LIVE OAK

16. OYSTER SHOAL

The males...are tall, erect, and moderately robust, their limbs well shaped, so as generally to form a perfect human figure; their features regular, and countenance open, dignified and placid; yet the forehead and brow so formed, as to strike you instantly with heroism and bravery; ...Their complexion of a reddish brown or copper colour; their hair long, lank, coarse and black as a raven, and reflecting the like lustre at different exposures to the light.

William Bartram, 1791

When they go to war against their enemies they bedaub their faces with all kinds of colors which they think best for giving them a frightful appearance. ...Their dwellings are little huts covered with bark or skins, under which they lie around by a good fire. They often change their domicile and consider human life too short for building houses. ...They speak little, answer briefly, observe everything and think all the more. ...Formerly they knew nothing of drunkeness, but since then they have learned this as well as other vices from the neighboring Christians.

Philip Georg Friedrich von Reck, May 1736

Archaeological evidence suggests that native Americans were living on these islands as early as 2500 B.C. Blessed by a pleasant climate and an abundance of game, seafood, and waterfowl, the Indians the Spanish came to call Guale lived relatively unstructured, seminomadic lives. Oysters were a staple in their diets, and great prehistoric mounds of discarded shells, called shell middens, still dot the Georgia coast. The Indians were decimated by Euro-pean diseases, and their values were debauched by foreign customs and spirits. Eventually they were over-whelmed by the rising tide of land-hungry immigrants. As members of the great Creek Confederacy, some tribes cooperated with the whites while others resisted. Hostilities flared on the coast into the late eight-eenth century, but a series of trea-ties and land cessions had removed all coastal Indians by 1812.

17. SHELL RING, CA. 1,500 B.C., SAPELO ISLAND

28

18. WHITE IBIS

Afayre coast, stretchyng of a great length, covered with an infinite number of high and fayre trees. (The waters) were boyling and roaring through the multitude of all kind of fish. (The land was the) fairest, fruitfullest, and pleasantest of all the world, abounding in hony, venison, wilde foule, forests, woods of all sorts, Palm trees, Cypresse, and Cedars, Bayes ye highest and greatest, with also the fayrest vines in all the world, with grapes according, which, without natural art and without man's helpe or trimming, will grow to toppes of Okes and other trees that be of a wonderfull greatnesse, and height. And the sight of the faire medowes is a pleasure not able to be expressed with tongue: full of Hernes, Curlues, Bitters, Mallards, Egrepths, Wood-cocks, and all other kinds of small birds: with Harts, Hindes, Buckes, wilde Swine, and all other kindes of wilde beastes, as we perceived well, both by their footing there, and also afterwardes in other places by their crie and roaring in the night.

To be short, it is a thing unspeakable to consider the thinges that bee seene there, and shal be founde more and more in this incomperable lande, which, never yet broken with plough yrons, bringeth forth al things according to his first nature wherewith the eternall God indued it.

THE TRUE AND LAST DISCOVERIE OF FLORIDA MADE
BY CAPTAIN JOHN RIBAULT IN THE YEERE 1562.

French Captain Ribault sailed the waters off the coast of what he referred to as northern Florida and gave the names Seine and Gironde to the rivers now known as the St. Marys and the Savannah. In 1566, the Spanish tried to establish Jesuit missions on the coast, but were soon forced to abandon the efforts because of the hostile activities of the local Indians. Later, Franciscan missions were more successful, but tensions with the Indians never entirely ceased during Spanish occupation. Traditionally, many of the tabby ruins that are scattered about the Georgia coast have been ascribed to Spanish mission efforts. There is, however, no current evidence to support this theory.

19. BEACH, OSSABAW ISLAND

20. SITE OF FORT KING GEORGE, 1721, DARIEN

July 13: I ordered the People to Row 3 miles down to this pleasant point, where they unloaded the Boats, and pitched the four Tents I brought with me, and the Indians field being grown up with Small Bushes, they Set the Same on fire and cleared a good way Round...that night...made all the men merry drinking His Majesty's and Your Excellency's Health.

July 14: I sett all hands at work, gott the great guns ashore, and mounted them, gott the mill, the grindstone, and the smiths or Armorers tools up, some grinding the tools, others helving the axes etc. and in short made a good dayes work.

July 17: Now there being no wood or Timber, within three miles of this it was impracticable to build anything of a Redoubt or small fort but with plank, and the most convenient place for cypruss is also 3 miles off. This cypruss can't be gott out of the swamp without wading naked up to the waist or sometimes to the neck, which is a terrible slavery, and especially now in the dog days, when musketos are in their vigor;.

Colonel John Barnwell, 1721

Although the missions had been largely unsuccessful, Carolina was still wary of the Spanish threat to the south. This, coupled with the continued troubles with the Indians and the possibility of French incursion, made it imperative that England stabilize the southern frontier. England responded to the pleas of the Carolinians by establishing an outpost near the mouth of the Altamaha River. The fort was to be built at the expense of Carolina and was begun in 1721. The site was unhealthy and very unpopular, however, and the fort was abandoned in 1727. The remains of the more than 140 men who perished while serving there are buried on the fort site near Darien. The only surviving virgin cypress in coastal Georgia—huge trees perhaps 1,500 years old—are on Lewis Island, a remote, state-protected swamp in the Altamaha basin.

21. BALD CYPRESS, LEWIS ISLAND

22. MOUTH OF THE SAVANNAH RIVER

To the Trustees for establishing the Colony of Georgia in America.

GENTLEMEN,—I gave you an Account in my last of our Arrival at Charles-Town. The Governor and Assembly have given us all possible Encouragement. Our People arrived at Beaufort on the 20th of January where I lodged them in some new Barracks built for the Soldiers, while I went myself to view the Savannah River. I fix'd upon a healthy situation about ten miles from the sea. The River here forms a Half-Moon, along the South-Side of which the Banks are about forty Foot high, and the Top a Flat which they call a Bluff. The plain high Ground extends into the Country five or six Miles, and along the River-side about a Mile. Ships that draw twelve Foot Water can ride within ten Yards of the Bank. Upon the River-Side, in the Centre of this Plain, I have laid out the Town. ...The River is pretty wide, the Water fresh, and from the Key of the Town you see its whole Course to the Sea, with the Island of Tybe, which forms the Mouth of the River; and the other way you see the River for about six Miles up into the Country. ...The whole People arrived here on the first of February. At Night their Tents were got up. 'Til the seventh were taken up in unloading and making a Crane which I then could not get finish'd, so took off the Hands, and set some to the Fortification and began to fell the woods. I mark'd out the Town and Common. Half of the former is already cleared, and the first House was begun Yesterday in the Afternoon. ...Mr. Whitaker has given us one hundred Head of Cattle. Col. Bull, Mr. Barlow, Mr. St. Julian, and Mr. Woodward are come up to assist us with some of their own Servants. ...A little Indian Nation, the only one within fifty Miles, is not only at Amity, but desirous to be Subjects to his Majesty King George, to have Lands given them among us, and to breed their Children at our Schools. Their Chief, and his Beloved Man, who is the Second Man in the Nation, desire to be instructed in the Christian Religion.

I am, Gentlemen
Your Most Obedient, Humble Servant,

James Oglethorpe.
February 10, 1733 (old style)

23. STATUE OF JAMES EDWARD OGLETHORPE, CHIPPEWA SQUARE, SAVANNNAH

34

24. REYNOLDS SQUARE, SAVANNAH

Each Free-holder has a Lott in Town 60 Foot by 90 Foot, besides which he has a Lott, beyond the Common of 5 Acres for a Garden. Every ten Houses make a Tything, and to every Tything there is a Mile Square, which is divided into 12 Lotts, besides Roads; ...Each Free-holder of the Tything has a Lott or Farm of 45 Acres there. ...Every 40 Houses in Town make a Ward to which 4 Square Miles in the Country belong; ...Where the Town-Lands end, the Villages begin; four Villages make a Ward without, which depends upon one of the Wards within the Town. The use of this is, in case a War should happen that the Villages without may have Places in the Town, to bring their Cattle and Families into for Refuge, and to that Purpose there is a Square left in every Ward big enough for the Out-Wards to encamp in.

Francis Moore, 1736

The city is laid out with the greatest regularity, the streets running in parallel lines with the river from east to west, and these crossed by others at right angles running north and south. Philadelphia itself is not more perfect in its symmetry than Savannah; and the latter has the advantage over the former, that there are no less than eighteen large squares, with grass-plots and trees, in the very heart of the city, ...Even now, in February...the prospect up and down every street in the city, intersected as it is by squares and rows of trees, is peculiarly pleasing.

James Silk Buckingham, 1839

25. HANOVER SQUARE, BRUNSWICK

The town that Oglethorpe laid out on the high bluff overlooking the Savannah River is remarkable not only because it is one of the few planned cities in America, but also because the integrity of the original plan was maintained as the city expanded. Oglethorpe designed similar plans for the towns of Ebenezer, Frederica, and Darien, and others imitated his ideas at Sunbury, Hardwicke, and Bruns-wick, but only Savannah has seen its early scheme reach maturity. The shade trees that fill the squares and line the streets of this early concept are a pleasant contrast to the busy reality of most modern cities, and as a result Savannah is widely known as one of the most beautiful cities in the nation. In recognition, an area of more than two square miles has been designated a National Historic Landmark District.

26. VERNON SQUARE, DARIEN

27. 426 EAST ST. JULIAN STREET, 1845, SAVANNAH

Savannah is about a mile and a quarter in Circumference; it stands upon the flat of a Hill; the Bank of the River (which they in barbarous English call a Bluff) is steep, and about 45 Foot perpendicular, so that all heavy Goods are brought up by a Crane, an Inconvenience designed to be remedied by a bridged Wharf, and an easy Ascent,...

The Town of Savannah is built of Wood; all the Houses of the first 40 Free-holders are of the same Size with that Mr. Oglethrope lives in, but there are great Numbers built since, I believe 100 to 150, many of these much larger, some of 2 or 3 Stories high, the Boards plained and painted.

Their Houses are built at a pretty large Distance from one another for fear of Fire; the Streets are very wide, and there are great Squares left at proper Distances for Markets and other Conveniences. Near the River-side there is a Guard-house inclosed with Palisades a Foot thick, where there are 19 or 20 Cannons mounted, and a continual Guard kept by the Free-holders.

There is near the Town to the East, a Garden belonging to the Trustees, consisting of 10 Acres, the situation is delightful, one half of it is upon the Top of a Hill, the Foot of which the River Savannah washes, and from it you see the Woody Islands in the Sea.

Francis Moore, Savannah, 1736

28. 510 EAST ST. JULIAN STREET, 1797, SAVANNAH

The first dwellings for Oglethorpe's settlers were temporary—tents and thatched huts—but the new Georgians immediately began constructing houses about the town Oglethorpe had so carefully planned. These first houses were all built of wood and to the same dimensions, "24 foot in length upon 16 foot in breadth." Soon more substantial homes, public and commercial buildings, and churches were erected. None of the early eighteenth-century structures have survived the fires, decay, and "progress" of the subsequent years, but there are several small houses in Savannah which were built later in the same scale and simple design as those early homes in the youngest colony.

29. 404 EAST BRYAN STREET, 1821-23, SAVANNAH

30. HEBREW CONGREGATION MICKVE ISRAEL, 1876-78, SAVANNAH

Washington, May 12, 1789
To the Hebrew Congregation of the City of Savannah, Ga.:

GENTLEMEN,—I thank you with great sincerity for your congratulations on my appointment to the office, which I have the honor to hold by the unanimous choice of my fellow citizens, and especially the expressions you are pleased to use in testifying the confidence that is reposed in me by your Congregation.

I rejoice that a spirit of liberality and philanthropy is much more prevalent than it formerly was among the enlightened nations of the earth, and that your brethren will benefit therby in proportion as it shall become still more extensive.

May the same wonder-working Deity who long since delivered the Hebrews from their Egyptian oppressors, planted them in a promised land, whose providential agency has lately been conspicuous in establishing these United States, as an independent nation, still continue to water them with the dews of heaven, and make the inhabitants of every denomination participate in the temporal and spiritual blessings of that people whose God is Jehovah.

George Washington

31. JEWISH COMMUNITY CEMETERY, 1773, SAVANNAH

The first Jewish families immigrated to Savannah in 1733, and, although many moved to South Carolina when Georgia became involved in the conflict between England and Spain, several families stayed on and had important roles in the development of the colony. The congregation Mickve Israel was formed in 1735 and currently holds services in a gothic revival synagogue constructed in 1876. The Hebrew Congregation was the only Savannah group to send a letter of congratulations to George Washington when he became president in 1789. The author of the letter, Levi Sheftall, was a member of a prominent Savannah family whose early high-walled cemetery stands on the west side of town.

32. EBENEZER CREEK, EFFINGHAM COUNTY

The Lands are inclosed between two Rivers, which fall into the Savannah. The Salzburg Town is to be built near the largest, which is called Ebenezer, ...and is navigable, being twelve Foot deep. The sweet Zephyrs preserve a delicious coolness notwithstanding the scorching Beams of the Sun. There are very fine Meadows, in which a great Quantity of Hay might be made with very little Pains. The Earth is so fertile that it will bring forth anything that can be sown or planted in it; whether Fruits, Herbs, or Trees. As to Game, here are Eagles, Wild-Turkies, Roe-Bucks, Wild-Goats, Stags, Wild-Cows, Horses, Hares, Partridges, and Buffaloes.

Philip Georg Friedrich von Reck, 1734

Old Ebenezer, where the Salzburgers settled at first, lies twenty-five miles west of Savannah. ...But the soil is a hungry, barren sand; and upon any sudden Shower, the Brooks rise several Feet perpendicular, and overflow whatever is near them. Since the Salzburgers remov'd, two English Families have been placed there; but these too say, That the Land is good for nothing; and that the Creek is of little Use; it being by Water twenty miles to the River; and the Water generally so low in Summer-time, that a Boat cannot come within six or seven miles of the Town.

Reverend Mr. John Wesley, 1737

The Salzburger immigrants who settled at Ebenezer were but a tiny handful of the thousands of Lutherans expelled from their homeland by the Catholic Archbishop Leopold. The original thirty-seven settlers, under the conduct of Mr. von Reck, arrived at Savannah in March 1734. Von Reck, awed by the lush landscape, was not practical when he chose the original town site, and, soon after the Salzburgers settled, they began to realize the inadequacies of the location. In 1736, strengthened by new arrivals from Europe, they moved to a new site at Red Bluff on the Savannah River. New Ebenezer, although populated by as industrious and able-bodied a group of settlers as any in the colony, was also ill-fated. The town suffered terribly at the hands of the British and Tories during the Revolution and never fully recovered. Jerusalem Church still stands, and services are held regularly, but the scar of a musket ball mars the swan atop the steeple, a small reminder of the turning point in the brief history of the old town.

33. JERUSALEM CHURCH, 1769, NEW EBENEZER

42

35. CHRIST EPISCOPAL CHURCH, 1838, SAVANNAH

34. CATHEDRAL OF ST. JOHN THE BAPTIST, 1872-76 (REBUILT 1898), SAVANNAH

The Colonists were from different nations, possessed widely variant characters and represented differing religions, creeds and governments. There were Swiss from the mountains, Piedmontese from the silk-growing districts of Lombardy; Germans from the archbishopric of Salzburg, Moravians from Herrnhut, Jews from Portugal, Highlanders from Scotland and English from London and circumjacent counties. There was the mercurial Italian, the reflecting Swiss, the phlegmatic German, the solemn Moravian, the blithesome yet hardy Scotchman, and the tame and depressed Briton. There too was seen the priest of the Church of England, the minister of the Presbyterians, the bishop and elders of the United Bretheren, pastors of the Lutheran and the ancient service of creeds; and like the ancient "mundus" of the Romans, each colonist seems to have brought, if not his native earth, at least his peculiar habits, customs and feelings, out of which time and, intercourse were destined to educe social union and provincial strength.

The Reverend William Baker Stevens, M.D., 1847

36. JONES CREEK BAPTIST CHURCH, 1856, ORGANIZED 1810, NEAR LUDOWICI

Early coastal areas naturally had a more diverse population than their inland neighbors because most commerce and travel was by sea. The English Trustees sent a variety of immigrants to Georgia—of the 1,847 colonists sent in the first ten years, only 1,008 were British. Similarly, many different denominations were represented, and their churches and meeting-houses have withstood the brutalities of time better than any other type of building. The beauty and strength of coastal churches is reflected in a wonderful variety of sizes and styles, from the plain and functional Baptist church at Jones Creek, near Ludowici, to the tall gothic spires of the Cathedral of St. John the Baptist in Savannah.

37. METHODIST CAMPGROUND, CA. 1790, TABERNACLE 1905-10, SPRINGFIELD

38. FORT FREDERICA, CA. 1740-41, ST. SIMONS ISLAND

On the 7th a party of their's marched toward the Town: our rangers discovered them and brought an account of their march, on which I advanced with a party of Indians, Rangers, and the Highland Company.

General Oglethorpe, 1742

These detachments having formed a junction observed at a distance the Spanish army on the march; and taking a favorable position near a marsh, formed an ambuscade. ...The enemy fortunately halted within a hundred paces of this position, stacked their arms, made fires, and were preparing their kettles for cooking, when a horse observed some of the party in ambuscade, and, frightened at the uniform of the regulars, began to snort, and gave the alarm. The Spaniards ran to their arms, but were shot down in great numbers by Oglethorpe's detachment, who continued invisible to the enemy; and after repeated attempts to form, in which some of their principal officers fell, they fled with the utmost precipitation, leaving their camp equipage on the field, and never halted until they got under cover of the guns of their battery and ships. ...So complete was the surprise of the enemy many fled without their arms; others in a rapid retreat discharged their muskets over their shoulders at their pursuers; ...From the signal victory obtained over the enemy, and the great slaughter amongst the Spanish troops, the scene of action just described has ever since been denominated the bloody marsh.

Captain McCall, 1742

39. BARRACKS, FREDERICA, CA. 1741-42, ST. SIMONS ISLAND

In 1736, Oglethorpe established the town of Frederica on St. Simons Island. This settlement and other English outposts south of the Altamaha River provoked the Spanish toward invasion of the Georgia coast. In 1738, war broke out between England and Spain; in 1740 Oglethorpe led an unsuccessful expedition against St. Augustine; and in 1742 the Spanish sent an armada and five thousand men to attack St. Simons. On July 7, 1742, the Spaniards were ambushed and routed at the Battle of Bloody Marsh. A few days later, confused and deluded by the boldness of Oglethorpe's maneuvers, they withdrew to Florida, unaware that they outnumbered the opposing troops eight to one. There were further threats of Spanish invasion in the following years before hostilities ceased with the Peace of Aix-la-Chapelle in 1748.

40. BLOODY MARSH, ST. SIMONS ISLAND

41. MCINTOSH SUGAR MILL, 1825, CAMDEN COUNTY

I was born in the old town of Frederica, in one of these Tabby houses; I had seen time destroy everything but them; I had seen them even sawed up into blocks, like a mass of living stone; and of such blocks, carried from Frederica, are the three first stories of the light-house at St. Simon's built. ...General Oglethorpe, doubtless, borrowed this mode of building from his neighbours, the Spaniards, but adapted it to the means he had in this country.

From the causes assigned above, the first house of any magnitude, I erected twenty odd years ago, I built of Tabby, and in this way. I was myself, I must acknowledge, astonished at the facility of the work, and the small expenditure of labour that was required; a massy building grew up under the labour of six black men and two boys, and mules, in a few months. They collected their own shells, burnt their own lime, mixed their mortar, consisting of equal parts of oyster shells, lime and sand, removed and filled their boxes—all the art that was necessary was to know the use of the plummet and the level, to keep the walls strait and perpendicular.

The process of our labour between March and July, (when only, such work should be carried on,) was to be two days in the week employed in collecting shells and building lime kilns, and four other days in the week in finishing two rounds, or two feet of walls, partitions and all.

On the mode of Constructing Tabby Buildings, and the propriety of improving our plantations in a permanent manner, *by Thomas Spalding*, The Southern Agriculturist, *December 1830*.

42. FORT WIMBERLY, CA. 1740-44, ISLE OF HOPE

43. HORTON HOUSE, 1740, JEKYLL ISLAND

44. SLAVE CABIN, CA. 1820, SAPELO ISLAND

Local Indians feasted on the plentiful oysters that lined the coastal riverbanks, and through the centuries they heaped the discarded shells into great piles now known as shell middens. Early European settlers recognized these middens to be an abundant resource and developed a building material called tabby. This substance was used in such early buildings as Fort Wymberly at Wormsloe and the Horton House on Jekyll Island. Thomas Spalding revived the practice of making tabby about 1810 when he employed it in the construction of his home on Sapelo Island. Spalding published his methods for the benefit of other planters, and in the next few decades many coastal structures, including slave cabins and sugar mills, were built of this durable material.

45. MIDWAY CHURCH, 1792, MIDWAY

Sir,—You cannot be ignorant that four armies are in motion to reduce this Province. One is already under the guns of your fort, and may be joined, when I think proper, by Colonel Prevost who is now at the Midway Meeting-House. The resistance you can, or intend to make will only bring destruction upon this country. On the contrary, if you will deliver me the fort which you command, lay down your arms, and remain neuter until the fate of America is determined, you shall, as well as all of the inhabitants of this parish, remain in peaceable possession of your property. Your answer, which I expect in an hour's time, will determine the fate of this country, whether it is to be laid in ashes, or remain as above proposed.

I am Sir, Your most obedient, etc., *L. V. Fuser,*
Colonel 60th Regiment, and Commander of his Majesty's
troops in Georgia, on his Majesty's Service.

Fort Morris, November 25, 1778.

Sir,—We acknowledge we are not ignorant that your army is in motion to endeavour to reduce this State. We believe it entirely chimerical that Colonel Prevost is at the Meeting-House; but should it be so, we are in no degree apprehensive of danger from a junction of his army with yours. We have no property compared with the object we contend for that we value a rush; and would rather perish in a vigorous defence than accept of your proposals. We, Sir, are fighting the battles of America, and therefore disdain to remain neutral till its fate is determined. As to surrendering the fort, receive this laconic reply:
COME AND TAKE IT. ...

I have the honor to be, Sir, Your most obedient Servant,
John McIntosh, Colonel of Continental Troops.

46. GWINNETT HOUSE, CA. 1765, ST. CATHERINES ISLAND

The outspoken, independent citizens of St. John's and St. Andrews parishes paid dearly for their devotion to the cause of Liberty, as the invading British troops burned their homes and churches and looted their farms in retribution. The house on St. Catherines Island, which is known by tradition as the home of Button Gwinnett, is the only one from that era to have survived. The old Midway Meeting House, the cradle of freedom in Georgia, was burned by the British in 1778. The current structure was erected in 1792 and is maintained by descendants of the original families.

47. SWAMP, LONG COUNTY

His name was a terror to the Tories. One of them, a man of considerable means, offered a reward of one hundred guineas to any person who would bring him the head of Robert Sallette. The Tory had never seen Sallette, but his alarm was such that he offered a reward large enough to tempt to assassinate the daring partisan. When Sallette heard of the reward, he disguised himself as a farmer, and provided himself with a pumpkin, which he placed in a bag. With the bag swinging across his shoulder, he made his way to the house of the Tory. He was invited in, and deposited the bag on the floor beside him, the pumpkin striking the boards with a thump.

"I have brought you the head of Robert Sallette," said he. "I hear that you have offered a reward of one hundred guineas for it."

"Where is it?" asked the Tory.

"I have it with me," replied Sallette, shaking the loose end of the bag. "Count me out the money and take the head."

The Tory, neither doubting nor suspecting, counted out the money, and placed it on the table.

"Now show me the head," said he.

Sallette removed his hat, tapped himself on the forehead, and said, "Here is the head of Robert Sallette!"

The Tory was so frightened that he jumped from the room, and Sallette pocketed the money and departed.

Joel Chandler Harris, 1886
STORIES OF GEORGIA

48. MONUMENT TO SGT. JASPER, MADISON SQUARE, SAVANNAH

The Revolution in Georgia generated its share of patriotic leaders and romantic heroes. Noble Wymberly Jones of Savannah was such an outspoken radical that Governor Wright thrice dissolved the provincial assembly rather than have Jones seated as its speaker. Archibald Bulloch, John Houstoun, and the brothers James and John Habersham were other prominent Savannah radicals. Several members of the famous McIntosh family, most notably Lachlan and John, served the Colonies with great distinction during the Revolution. Robert Sallette prowled the swamps of St. Johns Parish, terrorizing and confounding the Tories in his domain, and providing countless opportunities for later storytellers to expand on his exploits. The monument in Madison Square in Savannah commemorates the story of Sergeant Jasper, who is said to have been mortally wounded while retrieving the colors of his regiment.

49. EGRETS

How gently flow thy peaceful floods, O Altamaha! How sublimely rise to view, on thy elevated shores, yon Magnolian groves, from whose tops the surrounding expanse is perfumed, by clouds of incense, blended with the exhaling balm of the Liquid-amber, and odours continually arising from circumambient aromatic groves of Illicium, Myrica, Laurus, and Bignonia.

The air was filled with the loud and shrill whooping of the wary sharp-sighted crane. Behold, on yon decayed, defoliated Cypress tree, the solitary wood-pelican, dejectedly perched upon its utmost elevated spire; he there, like an ancient venerable sage, sets himself up as a mark of derision, for the safety of his kindred tribes. The crying-bird, another faithful guardian, screaming in the gloomy thickets, warns the feathered tribes of approaching peril; and the plumage of the swift sailing squadrons of Spanish curlews (white as the immaculate robe of innocence) gleam in the cerulean skies.

Thus secure and tranquil, and meditating on the marvellous scenes of primitive nature, as yet unmodified by the hand of man, I gently descended the peaceful stream, on whose polished surface were depicted the mutable shadows from its pensile banks; whilst myriads of finny inhabitants sported in its pellucid floods.

William Bartram, 1776

50. MAGNOLIA GRANDIFLORA

51. OSPREY

The marvelous reports of the first explorers and the verdant semi-tropical reality of coastal Georgia intrigued naturalists and collectors from the northern colonies and Europe. The fertile swamps and marshes were home to plants and animals considered wildly exotic to most of the world in the eighteenth century. Mark Catesby had explored the region in 1722, and after colonization many others made their way south to this fascinating frontier.

William Bartram and his son John documented the rare white flowered Franklinia and were the last people to see it bloom in the wild. Although egrets, herons, osprey, alligators, and even the bald eagle may still be seen in much the same habitats that existed in those innocent days, some of the reports and drawings of these adventurous men now tease us as melancholy reminders of the fragile balance of our coastal environment.

52. ALLIGATOR

54

53. WISTERIA

Every day after his breakfast he (Louis) took his last cup of coffee, his second or third, in his hand, and walked about the garden, enjoying its beauty and neatness and giving minut directions for its care and improvement. His especial pride was four or five camellia trees—I say trees, for even then they were a foot in diameter and fifteen feet height.

Joseph LeConte

Were these trees possessed by any of the New York florists they would consider them an independent fortune. Imagine what a magnificent appearance they present in winter, completely covered from their summit to the ground, with thousands and thousands of flowers, expanded at one time, contrasting with their glossy dark green foliage. You might cut bushels of flowers from them without missing them. These, with the beautiful chinese azaleas, decorate our parlors so gorgeously in the months of December, January, and February that we have no reason to complain of winter being a gloomy season.

Ann LeConte Stevens, 1854

54. AZALEA

Following the Revolution, botanical explorers roamed this horticulturally rich region establishing collection gardens and branch nurseries on coastal plantations. Andre Michaux, the French botanist credited with importing many foreign plants to the southern landscape, established gardens near Charleston, South Carolina, in 1786. A similar garden was maintained by John Lyon on the plantation of Phineas Miller on Cumberland Island, and John Couper had an experimental garden at Cannon's Point on St. Simons Island. In Chatham County, the gardens of Jonathan Bryan and Thomas Young were praised by noted visitors. Near Riceboro, in the Bulltown Swamp, the remarkable Woodmanston Plantation of Louis LeConte was the site of an internationally known bulb and camellia garden. The site, off the old Fort Barrington Road that the Bartrams and other early naturalists traveled, is open to visitors.

55. BULLTOWN SWAMP, WOODMANSTON, LIBERTY COUNTY

56. RICE FIELD, HOFWYL, GLYNN COUNTY

In taking my first walk on the island, I directed my steps toward the rice mill, a large building on the banks of the river, within a few yards of the house we occupy. ...

Immediately opposite to this building is a small shed, which they call the cook's shop, and where the daily allowance of rice and corn grits of the people is boiled and distributed to them by an old woman, whose special business this is. There are four settlements or villages (or, as the negroes call them, camps) on the island, consisting of from ten to twenty houses, and to each settlement is annexed a cook's shop with capacious caldrons, and the oldest wife of the settlement for officiating priestess. ...

My walks are rather circumscribed, inasmuch as the dikes are the only promenades. On all sides of these lie either the marshy rice-fields, the brimming river, or the swampy patches of yet unreclaimed forest. ...

As I skirted one of these thickets today, I stood still to admire the beauty of the shrubbery. Every shade of green, every variety of form, every degree of varnish, and all in full leaf and beauty in the very depth of winter. The stunted dark-colored oak; the magnolia bay; ...the wild myrtle; ...most beautiful of all, that pride of the South, the magnolia grandiflora, whose lustrous dark green perfect foliage would alone render it an object of admiration, without the queenly blossom whose color, size, and perfume are unrivaled in the whole vegetable kingdom. ...

I should like the wild savage loneliness, if it were not for slavery.

Francis Ann (Fanny) Kemble, 1838

57. RICE MILL STACK, CA. 1820, BUTLER ISLAND, MCINTOSH COUNTY

58. OVERSEER'S HOUSE, HOFWYL, 1851, GLYNN COUNTY

Rice production had been attempted on a small scale in coastal Georgia from the earliest days of the colony, but it did not begin to flourish until 1752, when the prohibition of slavery was lifted. The monumental task of swamp clearing, dam building, and channel digging could never have been attempted without slave labor. Rice soon became the most significant crop in Georgia, and its production was the basis of a new coastal aristocracy. Following the abolition of slavery, however, the profitability of the low country method of rice production declined significantly, and rice gradually faded from the local economy. Some cleared swamps have now been reclaimed by nature, while others remain as wet, grassy plains used principally as wildlife refuges.

59. DIKE AT ABANDONED RICE FIELD, RICEBORO

60. RICHARDSON-OWENS-THOMAS HOUSE, 1818, SAVANNAH

Savannah, 6 May 1819

My dearest Julia,
...It was understood the President was not to be here till Monday next; but a Messenger sent to meet him & returned last Evening reports he is to be here tomorrow or Saturday at furthest. I wish for my own Part he was come & gone—as until then all Business Arrangements will be broken in upon.—Our House is quite in readiness for him. It is most tastefully & elegantly decorated & furnished—& seems to bring to the Recollection of all who have lately visited it—the House of Lord Grosvenour in the neighborhood of Chester & Liverpool.—M. Jay is fixing up a temporary Pavilion of very great Extent in the church square opposite to Andrew Low's offices for the Ball & supper Rooms. It is lined with red Baize or flannel with festoons & pilasters of white muslin. It is also most tastefully & elegantly done—& by candle Light will look most superbly. The president must be pleased with Savannah:-as in the whole Course of his extended Tour, he may be received at a more costly & splendid Rate; but no where with such pure & genuine Taste;-& Jay will begin to attain the preeminence which low Jealousy & perverted Judgment would not before award him.—

We have advertised the steam ship to make passage to York & to return here in order that I may get in readiness for her Return from this; ...I hope that you will not allow any foolish Apprehensions to prevent your going across with me; ...

Your affectionate
William (Scarbrough)

61. RICHARDSON-OWENS-THOMAS HOUSE,

In 1796, a devastating fire swept away much of Savannah, but, by 1799, the city had begun to rise from its ashes on the shoulders of a new era of port prosperity. Fortunes were made in the production and shipping of cotton, and wealthy Savannah merchants began erecting magnificent homes about the town. William Jay, a young English architect, was commissioned to design several mansions, including the houses of William Scarbrough and Richard Richardson. The growing city continued to attract notable visitors—in 1819, President James Monroe was entertained in the Scarbrough House, and, in 1825, the Marquis de Lafayette spoke to the citizens of Savannah from the porch of the Richardson (Owens-Thomas) House.

62. SCARBROUGH HOUSE, 1819, SAVANNAH

63. MIDWAY RIVER, SUNBURY

Without trade, destitute of communications, and visited more and more each season with fevers, Sunbury, for nearly thirty years, has ceased to exist save in name. Its squares, lots, streets, and lanes have been converted into a corn field. Even the bricks of the ancient chimneys have been carted away. No sails whiten the blue waters of Midway River save those of a miserable little craft employed by its owner in conveying terrapins to Savannah. The old cemetery is so overgrown with trees and brambles that the graves of the dead can scarcely be located after the most diligent search. Fort Morris is enveloped in a wild growth of cedars and myrtle. Academy, churches, market, billiard room, wharves, store-houses, residences, all gone; only the bold Bermuda covered bluff and the beautiful river with the green island slumbering in its embrace to remind us of this lost town. ...The same bold bluff,—the same broad expanse of marshes stretching onward to the confines of the broad Atlantic,—the same blue outlines of Colonel's island and the Bryan shore,—the same sea-washed beach of St. Catherine,—the same green island dividing the river as it ebbs and flows with ever restless tide,—the same soft sea-breezes,—the same bright skies,—the same sweet voices and tranquil scene which nature gave and still perpetuates,—but all else how changed! ...Strange that a town of such repute, and within the confines of a young and prosperous commonwealth, should have so utterly faded from the face of the earth!

Charles Colcock Jones, Jr. 1878

64. FORT MORRIS, CA. 1756, SUNBURY

Sunbury, a port that rivaled Savannah in trade and importance in early Colonial years, began to wither at the end of the Revolution and never recovered. In its short history, however, it was the home to many notable men and women. Among them were two signers of the Declaration of Independence, the first U. S. Minister to China and Japan, and two Georgia governors. The earthwork Fort Morris has been restored and is the site of an interpretive museum.

65. SUNBURY CEMETERY

66. OAK GROVE CEMETERY, ST. MARYS

St. Marys is a port of entry and post town on the St. Marys River, within six miles of the Atlantic Ocean. It is one of the most pleasant and healthy seaports in the Southern States—Malignant or Bilious fever being almost unknown. The town at present contains near 1,000 inhabitants who are distinguished for their industry and hospitality. At no seaport south of Charleston can all kinds of merchandise be bought as cheap as at this placae; her merchants making annual visits to New York from whence they obtain their supplies. The town has two commodious churches viz: Presbyterian and Methodist and a flourishing Academy.

The market is well supplied with fish, meats and vegetables. The finest oysters in the world can be obtained here in abundance. Fish are sold at the rate of ten cents a dozen; fat hens at $1.15 a dozen; eggs at twelve cents; superior beef at 3½ cents per pound; smoked or jerked beef is furnished in abundance at three; fresh pork and bacon at six and seven and a great variety of fruits and vegetables. ...

The river has a bar which can be entered at all times by vessels drawing 17 feet of water, there being more than 20 on the bar. During the embargo when Florida belonged to Spain, it is computed that there were more than 300 square rigged vessels in the river and harbor at once. At present time there are several sawmills on the river actively employed sawing all kinds of lumber.

I. C. Stiles, 1837

The Town of St. Marys was founded in 1787 on land that had been granted to Jacob Weed. As the southernmost town on the Georgia coast, at the very edge of the frontier, it was not surprisingly a site of turmoil, tension, and adventure. French Arcadians settled there in the eighteenth century after being driven from their homes in Nova Scotia. In 1799, the people of St. Marys joined other cities across the young nation by planting oak trees to mark the death of George Washington. In 1804, Aaron Burr visited St. Marys and stayed at the house of Archibald Clarke. Burr's extended southern vacation, which was centered at the St. Simons Island home of Major Pierce Butler, was an attempt to escape the clamor of the North at the notoriety he had gained by killing Alexander Hamilton in a duel.

67. WASHINGTON OAK, ARCHIBALD CLARKE HOUSE, ST. MARYS

68. MIDWAY CHURCH, 1792, MIDWAY

Where is another to be found like unto it upon the habitable globe? It stands sui generis in its isolated grandeur, like some mountain peak that lifts its head far above all the rest. Look at the record. Four governors. Two signers of the Declaration of Independence. Six Congressmen, two of whom were Senators. Six counties named after her, five after her illustrious men, and the sixth after her own self, and achieved by her own prowess. Eighty-two ministers of the gospel. Six college professors. Three professors in Theological Seminaries. Two University chancellors. Six Foreign missionaries. Two judges of superior courts. Three solicitors. Three presidents of Female Colleges. Two mayors of cities. One United States Minister to a Foreign country. Four authors and one authoress. One historian. ...

When we remember that this was a church of plain country people, located in a sickly and sparsely populated section; the church edifice forty by sixty feet, with a membership...during its entire existence of one hundred and thirteen years, being only seven hundred and fifty-two; when we remember what that church has accomplished and is still doing for the world, we are lost in wonder. The impress and influence of such a church upon the world must simply be beyond all human calculation. Eternity alone will be able to reveal the good done by that one church and community.

Dr. James Stacy, 1899

69. DORCHESTER PRESBYTERIAN CHURCH, 1854, DORCHESTER

70. FLEMINGTON PRESBYTERIAN CHURCH, 1852, FLEMINGTON

71. WALTHOURVILLE PRESBYTERIAN CHURCH, 1884, WALTHOURVILLE

The Midway District was settled in 1752 by a group of Congregational Puritans of New England stock who had emigrated from Dorchester, South Carolina. Bringing with them a large number of slaves and a thorough knowledge of coastal rice cultivation, they soon began to prosper and to exert a substantial influence on the politics, culture, and economy of the young colony. For a variety of reasons, however, the Midway families began to settle in satellite "retreats" about the county, and soon Walthourville, Flemington, Jonesville, and Dorchester were vital communities. Churches were erected, and the dissolution of this remarkable congregation had begun. The 1792 church building is well maintained, and every spring the grounds come alive once again as descendants gather faithfully to share a service and walk in the footsteps of their forebears.

72. FACTORS' WALK, 1857-59, SAVANNAH

One should see the multitude of bales accumulating in the warehouses and elsewhere, in order to form an idea of the extent to which it is produced—long trains of cars heaped with bales, steamer after steamer loaded high with bales coming down the river, acres of bales on the wharves, acres of bales at the railway stations.

William Cullen Bryant, 1843

Savannah is the most charming of cities, and reminds me of the "maiden in the green wood." It is even more than Charleston, an assemblage of villas, which have come together for company. In each quarter is a green market-place, surrounded with magnificent lofty trees, and in the centre of each verdant market-place leaps up a living fountain, a spring of fresh water gushing forth, shining in the sun, and keeping the green sward moist and cool. Savannah might be called "the city of the gushing springs." There cannot be in the whole world a more beautiful city than Savannah. Now, however, it is too warm. There is too much sand and too little water, but I like Savannah.

Frederika Bremer, 1851

When Eli Whitney perfected the cotton gin in 1793 while a guest at a plantation near Savannah, the southern economy went into an extraordinary boom. From a total yield of only one thousand bales in 1790, production of cotton in Georgia soared to more than 700,000 bales by 1860. The plantation system flourished, and the dependence on slave labor deepened. Savannah was the trading center for rice and cotton, and the grand five-story buildings that housed the factors' offices lined the river bluff for one mile. From the bridges that connected their offices to the bluff, the factors would practice their trade—inspecting the new cotton and shouting their bids above the din of the workers and drays. The community prospered, and the era saw the construction of many new public amenities, such as the fine cast-iron harbor light and the exotic Forsyth Park fountain.

73. HARBOR LIGHT, 1852, SAVANNAH

74. FORSYTH PARK FOUNTAIN, 1858, SAVANNAH

75. ANDREW LOW HOUSE, 1849, SAVANNAH

Feast of St. Valentine
Savannah, Georgia (1855)

This welcome day brought me a nice long letter from K. E. P., and she must know that I write from the most comfortable quarters I have ever had in the United States. In a tranquil old city, wide-streeted, tree-planted, with a few cows and carriages toiling through the sandy road, a few happy negroes sauntering here and there, a red river with a tranquil little fleet of merchant-men taking in cargo, and tranquil ware-houses barricaded with packs of cotton,—no row, no tearing northern bustle, no ceaseless hotel racket, no crowds drinking at the bar,—a snug little languid audience of three or four hundred people, far too lazy to laugh or applaud; a famous good dinner, breakfast etc, and leisure all morning to think and do and sleep and read as I like. The only place I stay in the States where I can get these comforts—all free gratis—is the house of my friend Andrew Low of the great house of A. Low and Co., Cotton Dealers, brokers, Merchants—what's the word? Last time I was here he was a widower with two daughters in England, about whom—and other two daughters—there was endless talk between us. Now there is a pretty wife added to the establishment, and a little daughter number three crowing in the adjoining nursery. They are tremendous men these cotton merchants.

William Makepeace Thackeray, 1855

76. CHAMPION HOUSE, 1844, SAVANNAH

The wealth generated by the growing cotton trade precipitated a building boom in coastal Georgia cities. Noted architects such as Irish-born Charles Cluskey and John Norris of New York were employed to design grand homes for the rich Savannah merchants, and developers built bold rows of high stoop townhouses around the city. In St. Marys the impact of trade was nothing like that in Savannah, but the improvement in commerce did enable some families to build fine homes like the Greek revival Orange Hall. The mark of "King Cotton" was seen predominantly in the port cities, however, for capital in rural areas was being used to buy more acreage and the slaves to work it. The planters were not conserving the land, and their dependence on slavery to clear and cultivate new fields was increasing. The plantation economy was firmly entrenched.

77. ORANGE HALL, 1838, ST. MARYS

78. RETREAT PLANTATION HOUSE RUINS, CA. 1790, ST. SIMONS ISLAND

A ll these operations of tanning, shoemaking, blacksmithing, carpentering, the threshing, winnowing, and beating of rice, and the ginning, cleaning and packing cotton, were watched with interest by us boys, and often we gave a helping hand ourselves. There was special interest in the ginning of cotton by foot and the threshing of the rice by flail, because these were carried on by great numbers working together, the one by women, and the other by men, and always with singing and shouting and keeping time with the work.

Joseph LeConte, Woodmanston Plantation

My charge contained five white families and 1000 slaves. ...My host Mr. Couper, at Hopeton, was a man of most uncommon ability and attainment. ...I was acquainted with the more cultivated class of Southerners.

The Reverend George F. Clarke

We generally got to Observation Pond just as the sun was rising, and then how beautiful Retreat was as we came into the yard! So clean, and everything in order, with such comfort everywhere. ...Retreat was a dear old place with the beautiful trees and flowers, and the view of the Atlantic and the Sound, with Jekyll, and two or three vessels at anchor.

Caroline Wylly (Couper), St. Simons Island

Plantation living varied greatly from place to place, even within the same region. Coastal Georgia had more than its share of sophisticated plantation owners, and the names Couper, Butler, King, LeConte, Jones, Spalding, Greene, and McAlpin were known not just in Georgia but throughout the country and in many instances overseas as well. For every fine seat of comfort and manners, however, there were many other small rude plantations which were the stages of daily fights for survival. Similarly, the treatment of slaves was often a function of two factors—the humaneness of the master and the economic health of the plantation. Under all conditions, however, southern planters saw slaves as valuable, productive property, and an element absolutely essential to the success of the plantation economy. The abolition of slavery meant certain financial ruin.

79. OAK ALLEY, CA. 1848, RETREAT PLANTATION, ST. SIMONS ISLAND

80. SLAVE CABINS, HAMILTON PLANTATION, CA. 1820, NOW HOUSE THE OFFICES OF THE CASSINA GARDEN CLUB, ST. SIMONS ISLAND

81. FORT MCALLISTER, 1861, BRYAN COUNTY

Well, genl'mens, I'se b'longs to de King fambly since my longest 'membrance. ...Well, when we heard 'Fo't Sumpta' surrender, all my young masters say we must go...Well, I went wid mas' Lord, cos when he was a boy he wus mostly wid me. At fust it wus nothin', but w'en we went to 'Furginny' de truble commence. You kno' I use ter cook fur him and kinder take care of him, cos I wus leetle de oldest. ...Well, any of you gen'lmen wot ben in de march from de vally to the place call 'Fredricksburg,' mus' kno' wot a time it wer'. ...De army marches on tell we cum to whar Mas' Lord say was 'Mary Hite.' ...W'en supper was ready I go to call mas' Lord. He cum an' eat he supper, but don't talk like mos' de times; w'en he thro' he look in de fire a long time. I ben busy washin' de dishes w'en all a sudden he say: "Neptune, a big fite to-morrow mornin', good mens will eat deir las' supper to-nite." ...Well, de nex' day I see de canon gwine by, an' de solders marching by, an' de gen'rals ridin' by, an' I know'd trouble wus com'in. ...Nite cum, but no Mas' Lord. ...Well, after it git good dark I lef' de supper by de fire to go look fur Mas' Lord. ...I crawl down de hill; ded mens was ev'ry wher'. ...Den I cum to a' officer laying on he face. ...I turn he face up so he could look in old Neptune's face, an' I say, "My young master—Mas' Lord, dis is old Neptune; supper is ready; I been waiting fur you—is you hurt bad?" But he never answer his old nigger—he, ...Lord have mercy—he was ded! I take him up in my arm. De shells bust an' de bullets rattle, but I ain't 'fraid dem. Mas' Lord, my young master, dey can't hurt him; and Old Neptune don't care.

Recollections of *Neptune Small* as told to *J. E. Dart*

82. FORT PULASKI, 1829-47, NEAR TYBEE ISLAND

83. FORT JACKSON, 1842, SAVANNAH

Although Fort Pulaski was taken by federal troops early in the war, most of coastal Georgia was spared direct conflict until Sherman's army arrived, capturing stubborn Fort McAllister finally in 1864. Scores of Georgians had gone off to serve the Confederacy, and many, like Captain Henry Lord King of Retreat Plantation, were killed on fields far from home. The concept of slavery cannot be defended, but there sometimes existed a genuine tenderness and devotion between master and slave. Neptune Small brought the body of Captain King home to Georgia and later joined King's brother Cuyler on the battlefield. Neptune Small is buried in the old Retreat Burying Ground at the Sea Island Golf Course.

84. FORT PULASKI GATE, 1829-47, NEAR TYBEE ISLAND

Friday, December 16th. About four in the afternoon we heard the clash of arms and noise of horsemen, and by the time Mother and I could get downstairs we saw forty or fifty men in the pantry, flying hither and thither, ripping open the safe with their swords and breaking open the crockery cupboards. ...

They broke open Mother's little worktable with an andiron, hoping to find money or jewelry. ...Failing to find treasure, they took the sweet little locks of golden hair that her mother had cut from the heads of her angel children near a half century ago, and scattering them upon the floor trampled them under their feet.

We finally found one man who made a little show of authority. ...Mother appealed to him, and he came up and ordered the men out.

It is impossible to imagine the horrible uproar and stampede through the house, every room of which was occupied by them, all yelling, cursing, quarreling, and running from one room to another in wild confusion. ...These men belonged to Kilpatrick's cavalry. We look back upon their conduct in the house as a horrible nightmare, too terrible to be true. ...

In the gray twilight of morning we looked out of the window and saw one man pacing before the courtyard gate between the house and the kitchen; and we afterwards found he had voluntarily undertaken to guard the house. In this we felt that our prayers had been signally answered.

Mrs. Mary S. Jones Mallard, Montevideo, 1864

85. BACON-FRASER HOUSE, 1839, HINESVILLE

86. GREEN-MELDRIM HOUSE, 1853, SAVANNAH

In May 1864, General Sherman led his troops into Georgia and commenced the infamous March to the Sea. After burning Atlanta and wreaking havoc across a sixty-mile path toward the coast, the Union Army entered Savannah in December. Sherman set up headquarters in the Charles Green mansion on Madison Square and on the twenty-second sent a telegram to President Lincoln presenting the City of Savannah as a Christmas gift. The march through Georgia was intended to take the war to the doorsteps and break the spirit of the civilian South. Sherman accomplished this goal, but the brutal campaign etched his name in the dark corners of many southern hearts. The Bacon and Jones families of Liberty County were but two of the thousands who were terrorized during the one-month occupation. The first glimpse of twentieth-century warfare was a sad episode in the history of coastal Georgia.

87. FIRST AFRICAN BAPTIST CHURCH, 1861, SAVANNAH

Yesterday afternoon about half past three o'clock, the ceremonies of laying the cornerstone of the First Bryan Baptist Church took place in the presence of a large assemblage of colored people and a few whites. ...Rev. H. W. Turner, the orator of the day was introduced. His address was interesting and instructive.

SAVANNAH MORNING NEWS, *October 14, 1873*

The Negro population of Liberty County, about sixty-five percent of the total numbers about nine thousand. Most of them own their land on which they grow cotton, cane and rice, but prices are low and money is scarce. Tuition (to Dorchester Academy) is often paid in poultry, vegetables or fat pine for starting fires. Eggs purchase postage stamps and sometimes appear in the collection plates in church and Sunday School. ... The class of '96 received their diplomas from the hand of Principal Foster, ...a new event was chronicled in the history of this school and of Liberty County. This was the first class of colored students that has ever graduated in this county. The baccalaureate sermon was preached in the Midway Congregational Church by the pastor, the Rev. A. L. DeMond. His subject was "Character, Conduct and Culture, the Foundations for Success in Life."

From reports to the American Missionary Association, *Reverend Floyd Snelson, Warren G. Waterman,* and *Reverend A. L. DeMond, 1896*

88. KING-TISDELL HOUSE, 1896, SAVANNAH

After the war, the Freedmen's Bureau was established to protect the recently gained rights of the former slaves. The American Missionary Society sent representatives to the South to open schools like the Dorchester Academy and to begin to educate the mostly illiterate Black population. The real foundation for survival, however, lay in the Black churches. Black preachers had been allowed to learn to read and write by the plantation owners, and after emancipation they were the natural leaders of Black society. The churches were the centers of Black social life and became the primary means of overcoming long-held feelings of inferiority. Then, as the churches made their way toward complete autonomy, they became the machinery for the early Black political movement. Many of these churches still stand as active memorials to those turbulent and uncertain years. The renovated King-Tisdell Cottage in Savannah houses a museum of Black history.

89. ST. CYPRIANS EPISCOPAL CHURCH, 1876, DARIEN

78

90. SAVANNAH COTTON EXCHANGE, 1886, SAVANNAH

Not an office on the Bay was vacant, and applications for accommodations there remained unsatisfied. For many years there was a waiting list of prospective water front tenants. Until quite recent years in the busy cotton season the Bay Street buildings were illuminated until midnight, as scores of clerks worked on the records, and the Cotton Exchange, built in 1886, was thronged with factors and exporters when the market reports came in from Liverpool and New York and New Orleans. Today the Exchange is distressingly deserted. It is saddening to recall that last year Savannah handled 150,000 bales of cotton, or hardly more than 6 per cent of its maximum record. But in 1888, and the twenty years that followed, the air was vibrant with commercial electricity. The pulse of the city beat with the strength of a young giant. Everyone believed without reservation that Savannah was at the open door to an era of unprecedented progress fifty years ago.

Reconstruction, with all its evils and bitter memories, was but a few years in the rear. Georgia had risen to its feet and was recovering rapidly. The entire South—they called it "The New South"—felt the thrill of a fresh life in agriculture, industrial developments were beginning, foreign commerce was expanding, domestic trade was increasing. One could hardly enter Savannah without sensing the unbounded faith its people felt in its future.

Thomas Gamble, SAVANNAH MORNING NEWS, 1938

91. FORSYTH PARK, SAVANNAH

Post-war coastal Georgia was a curious mix of desperation and optimism. The principal city, Savannah, had been left virtually intact while the outlying plantations were in chaos. Northern and European entrepreneurs continued to influence the Savannah economy and trade in cotton regained its vigor. The ornate Savannah Cotton Exchange was built in 1886, and many new homes and public projects were going up throughout the city. On the plantations life had changed, and under the new conditions cotton and rice production continued, but the confusion of new roles significantly reduced its efficiency. Wages had to be paid and more and more fertilizer bought to replenish a depleted soil. It became harder to compete with the productivity and prices of the more fertile lands to the west—the era of the coastal plantation was rapidly coming to an end.

92. HAMILTON HOUSE, 1873, SAVANNAH

94. VICTORIAN DETAIL, GASTON STREET, 1891-92, SAVANNAH

93. ASENDORF HOUSE, 1899, SAVANNAH

Now that the street railroad affords a speedy means of communication between the extreme northern and southern sections of the city, we hope to see an impetus given to the building of houses on the lots now lying open in the southern part of the city. A fine opportunity is now afforded to give Savannah an appearance of beauty which it has never before known, by the building of handsome cottage houses out in that section which shall not be too large for a small family nor too small for the moderate sized one; and houses which will suit the pecuniary resources of a class of people who are not by any means wealthy, but who in point of respectability, intelligence, etc. rank with the best. At present such persons have either to adopt the tenement system, and live two or three families in one house, or else take refuge in a boarding house.

SAVANNAH MORNING NEWS, *1869*

The city, regardless of the groans of the property owners, thrilled with expectations. Despite the outcries against taxes, building went merrily on. In the three years 1888-1890, a thousand buildings were erected and seven hundred remodeled or improved.

SAVANNAH MORNING NEWS, *1938*

The building mania continues...new buildings are going up, but we need dozens more.

Brunswick, 1881

95. VICTORIAN DETAIL, HABERSHAM STREET, 1898, SAVANNAH

Many families who were not able to return to their ruined farms after the Civil War migrated to urban centers like Savannah and Brunswick. This influx of population prompted an immediate need for housing and better transportation. The Victorian District in Savannah developed during this period and was a direct result of the establishment of a streetcar system in 1869. In Brunswick the population swelled six-fold in the two decades before 1900. Homes built during this era vary from the Romanesque revival designs in brick and terracotta by William Gibbons Preston and Alfred Eichberg to the more numerous brightly colored wooden houses with whimsical jigsaw decoration. Substantial homes were built during this period, but the major growth in home construction was for the less affluent. Building and loan associations enabled families of modest means to build frame houses with plans and details ordered right out of catalogs.

96. VICTORIAN DETAIL, BOLTON STREET, 1896, SAVANNAH

97. RABUN HOME, 1889, GUYTON

As we were traversing one of the (swamps), at the rate of half a mile an hour, I began to contrast the speed of the new railway with stage-traveling. Our driver maintained that he could go as fast as the cars. "How do you make that out?" said I. "Put a locomotive," he replied, "on this swamp, and see which will get on best." The most you can say is, that each kind of vehicle runs fastest on its own line of road.

Charles Lyell, 1849

There are about one thousand hands at work on the Waycross and Jacksonville Railway, and others being sought for and coming from all directions. Passenger trains and engines have been contracted for and are being constructed, to be delivered by December 1st—. ...The time from Jacksonville to New York will be made in through cars in thirty-six hours. Three daily passenger trains, via this route to Jacksonville—two from Savannah, and one from Macon. The roadway and equipment of this line will be first class in every respect, and the best that money can buy.

SAVANNAH MORNING NEWS, *August 29, 1880*

Some folks say that the Nancy Hanks can't run,
But stop, let me tell you what the Nancy done;
She left Atlanta at half past one,
And got to Savannah by the settin' o' the sun.

Doggerel, recounted by *Thomas Gamble, 1938*

98. STACK WITH PRIVIES, CENTRAL OF GEORGIA RAILROAD, CA. 1850, SAVANNAH

The Central of Georgia Railroad, built before the war, had linked Savannah with the cotton producing interior and had ensured the continued growth of the port. One of Sherman's priorities had been to destroy the Georgia rail system, thereby cutting supply lines and further retarding the economy. Rails were pulled and bent around trees—"Sherman's neckties" littered the landscape. Therefore, an immediate post-war task was to repair the damaged lines and replenish the rolling stock, while adding new roads to the system. These lines connected the coast with the timber producing interior. New towns such as Willie, Allenhurst, Ludowici, Cox, and Townsend all sprang up along the extensions of the railroads. Older communities such as Guyton in Effingham County, laid out in 1838, became summer retreats for Savannah businessmen once the railroads offered easy access to the city.

99. WELL PAVILION, 1907, LUDOWICI

100. CHRIST CHURCH, 1884, ST. SIMONS ISLAND

On this island is located the great saw mill, one of the largest in the world, of Dodge, Meigs & Co. of New York City, which manufactures lumber at the rate of 140,000 feet a day. There is a water way connection with nearly 300,000 acres of yellow pine forest that is penetrated by railroads to the extent of seventy-five miles, over which the great logs are transported to the rivers to be rafted to the big mill for manufacture into lumber. It is an immense industry, employing an army of men.

This is probably the largest establishment of the kind in the South. The company, besides owning 300,000 acres of pine land near Eastman, makes purchases of timber constantly from Darien and other points on the Altamaha River. At this time they have on hand awaiting shipment as fast as possible no less than four million feet of merchantable lumber, which will be sent to coastwise ports and South America as rapidly as it can be loaded. ...Sometimes no less than nine ships may be seen at their wharves receiving cargoes for every part of the world. ...They employ 150 hands and the payroll is about $3,000 per month. The cost of the plant was over $100,000. Quite a flourishing village has grown up around the mills, with a neat church, schoolhouse, post office and store. The population is about 300.

From newspaper accounts of the early 1880s

101. ST. JAMES UNION CHURCH (NOW LOVELY LANE CHAPEL), 1880, ST. SIMONS ISLAND

The most important element in the resurging coastal economy had been growing in the abundant swamps and forests all along, and great sawmills were started in Darien, St. Marys, and on St. Simons Island. Active communities of mill workers sprang up near the mills—complete with stores, infirmaries, and churches, like the St. James Union Church at the St. Simons Mills. Anson Dodge, of the New York family that opened the mills on St. Simons, became an Episcopal priest and de-voted his life to the resurrection and service of Christ Church at Frederica. Darien, Brunswick, St. Marys, and Savannah came to be great timber ports in the late nineteenth century, and groves of ships' masts could be seen at the docks as lumber was load-ed for shipment to distant countries. Many ship captains settled in the local communities and built com-fortable new homes, several of which may be seen at the Ridge near Darien.

102. DOWNEY HOUSE, 1882, THE RIDGE, NEAR DARIEN

103. MARSH SCENE, GLYNN COUNTY

S_{o:}

Affable live-oak, leaning low,-
Thus-with your favor-soft, with a reverent hand,
(Not lightly touching your person, Lord of the land!)
Bending your beauty aside, with a step I stand
On the firm-packed sand,
　　　　Free
By a world of marsh that borders a world of sea.
　　Sinuous southward and sinuous northward the
　　　　shimmering band
　　Of the sand-beach fastens the fringe of the marsh to
　　　　the folds of the land.
Inward and outward to northward and southward the
　　　　beach-lines linger and curl
As a silver-wrought garment that clings to and follows the
　　　　firm sweet limbs of a girl.
Vanishing, swerving, evermore curving again into sight,
Softly the sand-beach wavers away to a dim gray looping
　　　　of light.
And what if behind me to the westward the wall of the
　　　　woods stands high?
The world lies east: how ample, the marsh and the sea and
　　　　the sky!
A league and a league of marsh-grass, waist-high, broad in
　　　　the blade,
Green, and all of a height, and unflecked with a light or
　　　　a shade,
Stretch leisurely off, in a pleasant plain.
To the terminal blue of the main.
Oh, what is abroad in the marsh and the terminal sea?
　　Somehow my soul seems suddenly free
From the weighing of fate and the sad discussion of sin,
By the length and the breadth and the sweep of the
　　　　marshes of Glynn.

Sidney Lanier, from THE MARSHES OF GLYNN

104. BEACH, SEA ISLAND

105. LIVE OAK

106. BEACH, ST. SIMONS ISLAND

April 13. After a good night's rest and breakfast I enjoyed a lounge upon the piazza overlooking St. Simons Sound, and devoted the customary time to writing up my diary. To sojourners the island is almost "out of the world," so to speak, but it is a comfort to be where one can commune with nature and let the great, bustling, restless, discordant world, with its politics, its strife, its greatness, and littleness, take care of itself for a season. The mail is the connecting link that still keeps the recluse in touch with the outer world, however he may wish to forget it.

April 16. This day was to wind up our stay upon St. Simons Island. We had seen enough to convince us of the beauty of the place and its availability as a place of resort in winter; it needed but a hotel to make it popular.

> And now, far removed from that loved situation,
> Fond tears of regret will obtrusively flow,
> When memory recalls the St. Simon's diversion,
> And sighs for its pleasures wherever we go.
> That pleasant bright island,
> That sunshining island,
> That health-giving island,
> That lies by the sea.

Joseph W. Smith, 1883

107. MAHONEY-MCGARVEY HOUSE, 1891, BRUNSWICK

108. FREDERICA RIVER, GLYNN COUNTY

Although Sidney Lanier perhaps best expressed the marvelous beauty and salubrious effects of the coastal environment, many others were just as moved by their experiences here. The post-war economy provided Americans with greater leisure time and more disposable income, and better transportation facilities dramatically increased the accessibility of these island kingdoms-by-the-sea. In 1887, a rail line was completed from Savannah to Tybee Island, and, despite being served only by steam ferryboats, seaside hotels and guest cottages flourished on St. Simons. In Brunswick, the great Oglethorpe Hotel was built overlooking the East River and the marshes beyond. The hotel has been demolished, but a hint of its grandeur can be seen in the fantastic decoration of the Mahoney-McGarvey House, designed by the same architect, J. A. Wood.

109. DUNES, CUMBERLAND ISLAND

Away north runs up Cumberland Beach, and among the trees and over a broad stretch of marsh gleam white the ruins of "Dungeness." ...Here, for ages of time, the Indians of the South had resorted to feast upon the oysters with which the creek was filled. ...The summit of this shell-mound was levelled for the site of the house, and a terraced area of an acre or more constructed with the shells. Upon this base, raised above the general level of the island, its foundations were laid. It was four stories in height above the basement, and from cellar-stone to eaves was forty-five feet. There were four chimneys and sixteen fireplaces, and twenty rooms above the first floor. ...The garden lay to the south, reaching the marsh in successive terraces. On and about the semicircular terrace immediately around the house were planted crape-myrtle, clove trees, and sago palms. Some yet remain to indicate what an Eden-like retreat was this garden of spices and bloom half a century ago. ...It is one of the joys of the earth to walk through the Grand Avenue of Dungeness at sunset. ...

Three hundred feet in width, hard as stone, shell-strewn, between wind-hollowed sand-dunes and foaming surf, this beach of Cumberland stretches for twenty miles. ...They are called barren by many, these sandhills of the Atlantic coast, but I never find them so. ...So fascinating are these sand-dunes that one wanders among them for hours, following in the paths worn by the feet of cattle which roam these hills and the neighboring marsh in a half-wild state.

Frederick Albion Ober, LIPPINCOTT MAGAZINE, 1880

110. ISLAND HORSES AND DUNE, CUMBERLAND ISLAND

111. RUINS OF DUNGENESS, 1884, CUMBERLAND ISLAND

Cumberland, the largest and southernmost island on the Georgia coast, has a rich and fascinating history. In the early days of the colony, Oglethorpe built a hunting lodge on the south end of the island and named it Dungeness. The property was later acquired by Revolutionary War hero Nathanael Greene. He died before actually building there, but his widow and her new husband, Phineas Miller, moved to Cumberland and maintained an elaborate home with magnificent walled gardens. In 1880, Thomas Carnegie and his wife, Lucy, read an article about the Miller's Dungeness in Lippincott Magazine. The next year they purchased the property and built their own large house on the site of the earlier house. Later, their children also constructed fine houses on the island, including Greyfield, which is now an inn. Congress designated Cumberland a national seashore in 1972, and the National Park Service is now responsible for most of the island. A ferry transports day-trippers and campers to St. Marys on a regular schedule.

112. JEKYLL ISLAND CLUBHOUSE, 1888, JEKYLL ISLAND

I thank you for my two weeks at Jekyll Island. They were most enjoyable and how could they be otherwise, surrounded as I was with charming, well-bred people, with an interesting golf course, and men to play with whose keen interest in the game and spirit of fun made eighteen holes a real treat.

Then came a drive through those woodland groves, along that wonderful beach, and, after a good dinner, an evening before the wood fire in the smoking room, listening to men who have seen and done things; men with war experience and stories of hunting and yachting and traveling, here and in other lands, interspersed with wit and humor, and, think of it, no gossip. I, for once, did not miss the band and music and the dancing which are found in so many of our Southern watering-places. Those beautiful moonlight nights and the days when the air was filled with a perfume of flowers and the mocking-birds were singing in the trees, were much more to my taste, and when it came to Sunday, the services in the little Chapel, where eminent bishops and divines discoursed upon things which every thoughtful man is thinking about, suited me.

It is certainly a unique place. I know of no resort of its kind in this country or any other country. And when you see the tired men and women, who come there, restored to health and strength, you feel that there must be some combination of circumstances that makes the place so attractive and restoring. The real spirit of comradeship, which makes all, old and young, feel that they belong to the family, stimulates one to give of their best for the pleasure of others.

A visitor to the Jekyll Island Club

113. CRANE COTTAGE, 1916, JEKYLL ISLAND

114. MORGAN TENNIS COURT, 1929, JEKYLL ISLAND

In 1886, a group of northern investors formed the Jekyll Island Club, and the island underwent a remarkable transformation. A grand clubhouse and magnificent "cottages" were put up, tennis courts (including the Morgan indoor court) and a golf course were built, and a new pier was constructed for the mooring of some of the finest yachts in the world. The island became the winter destination of the most distinguished families of American industrial wealth, and the club register of those years shows the names Vanderbilt, Rockerfeller, Astor, Gould, and Morgan, among others. In 1947, the State of Georgia purchased the island and the wonderful "Millionaires' Village" is now open to the public.

115. GLYNN COUNTY COURTHOUSE, 1907, BRUNSWICK

It was 1927, and Mary Jones, Kate's and my cousin, got her daddy's car one day for us to go ride up to Midway. It was a Ford coupe, a very ancient coupe, and the radiator ran hot frequently. Uncle Maury had a lot of tin cans down on the floor and up in back of the seat, and he stopped at almost every ditch to fill up the radiator. Well, Mary wasn't prepared for it, exactly, and when we got nearly to Midway, the steam started pouring out. Mary screamed, "The car's on fire," and since Uncle Maury had wired the driver's door shut, she started climbing over me to get out. But she hadn't put on the brakes or anything, so there we were, three scared girls rolling down Mr. Granger's new road in a driverless car. I reached over and tried to put on the brakes, but all of those cans were rolling around down there, and I couldn't.

Kate got out on the running board, and, having always been very athletic, thought she could jump off running, but we were going too fast, and she fell and hit the concrete hard. Mary stayed on until we left the road, and then she jumped off. I was too much of a sissy, so I stayed in the car until it stopped in the ditch. I still don't remember who picked us up, but we went on to the Brownings in Midway.

Daddy and Papa Winn were on the highway commission and were going to be in the ceremonies to open the new road in October, but Kate dedicated the coastal highway that day and knocked all the skin off of one hip to christen it.

Cordella Jones Browning

116. GRAVE OF JULIETTE GORDON LOW, LAUREL GROVE CEMETERY, SAVANNAH

117. ARDSLEY PARK, 1910, SAVANNAH

The twentieth century brought sweeping changes but also a continuation of growth and tradition. Nourished by lumber production and tourist visitation, the economy of Glynn County remained healthy. As evidence of this, a handsome new courthouse was erected in Brunswick. Savannah, always cosmopolitan, was midwife to a movement of national significance when Juliette Gordon Low formed the first Girl Scout Troop in America in 1912. The advent of automotive transportation augured great changes as cities spread out, and suburban developments like Ardsley Park in Savannah became fashionable. To accommodate the newly independent traveler, coastal roads were paved, bridges built, and new hotels with better facilities constructed. Industrialist Howard Coffin built the Cloister Hotel on Sea Island, the focal point for his internationally known resort community.

118. THE CLOISTER HOTEL, 1928, SEA ISLAND

119. OFFICERS' ROW, FORT SCREVEN, CA. 1900, TYBEE ISLAND

The plan of the War Department to establish an anti-aircraft training base in Southeast Georgia turns on the acquisition by the federal government, via purchase or condemnation of the vastest tract of Crackerland that has changed ownership since the Cherokee Nation of Indians sold all of its immovable holdings in the 1820's preparatory to the trek of the tribe to the West.

Ralph Smith, ATLANTA JOURNAL, 1940

The War Department through the land acquisition facilities of the Soil Conservation Service, Department of Agriculture is now proceeding with the appraisal and purchase of lands for the site of the large anti-aircraft training and firing center to be located in parts of Liberty, Bryan, Long, Tattnall and Evans counties. ...Several towns and settlements located within the center will disappear with government acquisition of the property. They include Clyde, former county seat of Bryan county; Willie, Letford and Taylor's Creek, famous as a Methodist camp meeting site.

Buildings within the area, including schools, stores, and residences, will be razed, except such as are needed for use by the troops. The buildings to be razed or moved will be offered for sale by the government. ...As hearings began on the dispossession proceedings for the Camp Stewart firing center, Judge William H. Barrett said everything would be done for the assistance and comfort of those who have to vacate the land. ...While moving out of his own home was a hard matter for a man, Judge Barrett stated, it was better for the general welfare of the nation to have its defenses well set up so as to prevent a foreign invader attacking these homes.

SAVANNAH MORNING NEWS, 1940-1941

The importance of federal installations to the southern economy has been substantial, and certainly coastal Georgia has been a willing beneficiary. The large twentieth-century training bases and airfields require huge parcels of land, however, and entire communities were sometimes absorbed for the national welfare. When the anti-aircraft training facility of Camp (later Fort) Stewart was approved in 1940, many long-time residents had to be relocated. Today the military still plays an important role with the renewed growth of the Fort Stewart/ Hunter Army Airfield complex and the development of the Kings Bay Trident Nuclear Submarine Base near St. Marys.

120. GOULD CEMETERY,
HARRIS NECK, MCINTOSH COUNTY

121. TAYLORS CREEK CEMETERY, LIBERTY COUNTY

122. CLYDE CEMETERY, BRYAN COUNTY

123. COCKSPUR ISLAND AND LAZARETTO CREEK, CHATHAM COUNTY

Another boat that was a real part of our Island life was the shrimp trawler. We did not need alarm clocks because we were waked up at daylight every morning by these boats chugging along the shoreline on their way to the shrimp beds. When seining inside the harbor, they came close to the beach, moving along on the edge of the channel. They were so close, in fact, that our collie dog, Rab, met them at the end of the Colony and barked furiously as their motors broke the morning quiet. He ran in and out the water's edge until the boats left him behind then turned back to pick up another one and chase it.

We were never able to talk any of the captains of these trawlers into taking us out; and I am not sure it would have been as much fun as the pilot boat, because very few of these shrimpers spoke English.

They did not often stop at our dock because they sold all of their catch to the wholesale companies in Brunswick. But, when they did, Mother would give us fifty cents and we would race to catch them before they left. She loved the big shrimp they caught, and we could buy a peck for half a dollar. The boat's deck was usually covered with the jumping, slithering crustaceans. We never minded running this errand because everybody enjoyed a big platter of "prawn shrimp" fried, Betty style.

Frances Peabody McKay

124. DARIEN WATERFRONT

Seafood has been a naturally important ingredient of coastal diets since the first humans walked these shores, and shrimp, crabs, and oysters, while rare delicacies in many parts of the world, have always been plentiful in the waters of the Georgia coast. Modern pressures of river channelization and industrial growth have teamed with recent unusually hard winters to reduce the harvests, however, and local citizens have begun to realize just how fragile the ecological balance is. Georgia marshlands comprise some of the most productive acreage on the planet, and they are the nurseries for the bounty of seafood which has been long taken for granted. The shrimp boat fleets at Lazaretto Creek, Thunderbolt, Darien, and elsewhere along the coast are picturesque, but, more importantly, they are a barometer for the health of the precious marshlands. It is the responsibility of each generation to ensure that they remain a vital part of the coastal landscape.

125. THUNDERBOLT, CHATHAM COUNTY

126. SAVANNAH RIVER AND RIVER STREET

I got up early yesterday and watched Capt. Joe Myatt of the Atlantic Towing Co.'s tugboat Chatham dock two big ships and undock a third in Savannah's bustling harbor.

And I am ready to report that maneuvering one of those big ships in and around the tight spots along the riverfront looks to me about as easy as threading a needle up a dark alley in a rainstorm.

Capt. Myatt yesterday took his turn to act as "docking pilot," the fellow who gets a transfer in mid-stream from his tugboat to the visiting ship then twists and turns her neatly alongside a pier. ...

Because he got up even earlier than I did, Capt. Myatt and his crew and other tugboats brought in, or out, four ships altogether between about 7:00 a.m. and 3:30 p.m..

I got aboard in time to meet the American steamship African Rainbow, which rode high in the water from Baltimore. We climbed aboard and Capt. Myatt took over

With a series of toots on the whistle around his neck, the whistles on the tugs and the whistle on the African Rainbow, the 500 and some odd feet of ship was slowly turned 180 degrees in a 600-foot wide channel, then nimbly coaxed alongside the Atlantic Coast Line terminals.

In a matter of minutes the job is done. The lines are out and a ship is secured to the pier, ready to take on or discharge its cargo.

Arthur Whitfield, SAVANNAH MORNING NEWS, 1957

127. BRUNSWICK RIVER, GLYNN COUNTY

128. ISLE OF HOPE, CHATHAM COUNTY

In 1896, the Savannah harbor, including parts of the main shipping channel, was still littered with the wrecks of scuttled ironclads and other ships destroyed during the Confederate evacuation of Savannah. That year a twenty-four-foot channel was dredged and most of the obstructions were removed. Fertilizer, timber, refined sugar, cottonseed oil, cigars, and textiles began to replace the cotton and naval store shipments that had dominated the wharves for years. In 1945, the Georgia Ports Authority was formed, and since that time the port, with a thirty-eight-foot channel, has grown to be the largest in international commerce on the south Atlantic. The Port of Brunswick offers deepwater barge, railroad, and interstate highway access, making it an important bulk commodity port, and the opening of a terminal at Colonels Island further enhances the prospects of growth.

129. LAZARETTO CREEK, CHATHAM COUNTY

Moon River,
Wider than a mile:
I'm crossin' you in style
Some day.
Old dream maker,
You heart breaker,
Wherever you're goin',
I'm goin' your way:

Two drifters,
Off to see the world,
There's such a lot of world
To see.
We're after the same
Rainbow's end
Waitin' round the bend,
My huckleberry friend,
Moon River
And me.

Johnny Mercer
Copyright Famous Music Corporation, 1961

Johnny Mercer, the son of an old Savannah family, was a world-famous lyricist whose list of hits is astonishing, but perhaps his best-loved song was inspired by the winding Back River near his coastal home. To honor their native son, the local government later changed the name of the river to match the song.

The natural beauty and intriguing history of the Georgia coast have fired the imaginations of writers from Francis Goulding to Eugenia Price— even the unhappy Fanny Kemble's bitter words turned to sweetly flowing wonder when she described the coastal habitat.

130. GRIMBALL RIVER, CHATHAM COUNTY

131. DAVENPORT HOUSE, 1821, SAVANNAH

S avannah. Stately homes, shuttered against the afternoon sun. Quiet streets canopied with live oak and Spanish moss, magnolia and palmetto. ...

It hardly seems the setting for one of the most dramatic preservation stories in American history. Yet Savannah, grand and gentle lady of the Old South, has undergone a remarkable renaissance in the last two decades. The downtown area, once virtually abandoned, has become the nation's largest urban historic district, 2.2 square miles, comprising the central business district, the riverfront, and a number of residential neighborhoods, each with a wealth of splendid architecture. More than 800 buildings have been restored, and demolition has been brought to a virtual standstill. Now preservationists have turned their attention to another treasure: a 45-square-block neighborhood of Victorian homes, just south of the original historic district, that was built around the turn of the century as a middle-class suburb and now is badly dilapidated. The preservation movement has become a potent political force, if for no other reason than the money it generated: Property values in the historic district have soared, and tourism has grown from practically nothing to a $60-million-a-year industry.

Carol Matlack, AMERICAN PRESERVATION, 1979

Since the turn of the century, individuals, agencies, and organizations have spearheaded efforts to preserve historic sites along the coast. In 1903, the Colonial Dames acquired a part of the Frederica tract in order to preserve the colonial fort ruins from further destruction. From this beginning, great strides in historic preservation have been made, but the watershed of the movement was in 1955 when a group of concerned citizens banded together to save the Davenport House, and the Historic Savannah Foundation was born. Since then Savannah has been the prototype for such efforts, and many coastal communities have been able to save local treasures—often finding adaptive uses to justify obsolete but historic structures. For example, the Lighthouse Keeper's Cottage on St. Simons now houses the museum and archives of the Coastal Georgia Historical Society. Meanwhile, much of our forest and wetlands acreage has been maintained for timber production and wildlife habitats, and private interests retain many islands as retreats. Thus, landuse and ownership patterns have greatly contributed to efforts to protect much of coastal Georgia from overdevelopment. With continued good fortune and diligence, the natural beauty of coastal Georgia will be safeguarded for the enjoyment of future generations.

132. ST. SIMONS LIGHTHOUSE AND KEEPER'S HOUSE, 1872, ST. SIMONS ISLAND

133. PULASKI SQUARE, SAVANNAH

134. DEER

135. ABANDONED RICE FIELD, MCINTOSH COUNTY

136. RICE FIELD ON THE SATILLA RIVER, CAMDEN COUNTY

137. FLOWERING DOGWOOD

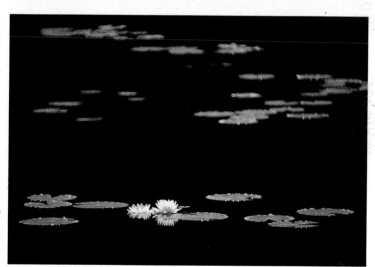

138. WATER-LILIES

139. RIVER STREET, SAVANNAH

140. FOURTH OF JULY, SAVANNAH

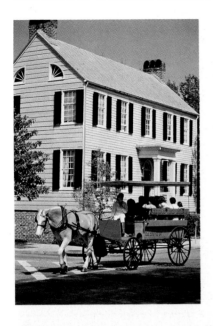

The maps provided on the following pages are intended to help the reader locate and visit the specific natural and historic sites pictured in this book. More detailed maps, additional site literature, and information on recreational activities and accommodations may be found at the various visitors' centers along the coast or by contacting the Coastal Area Planning and Development Commission.

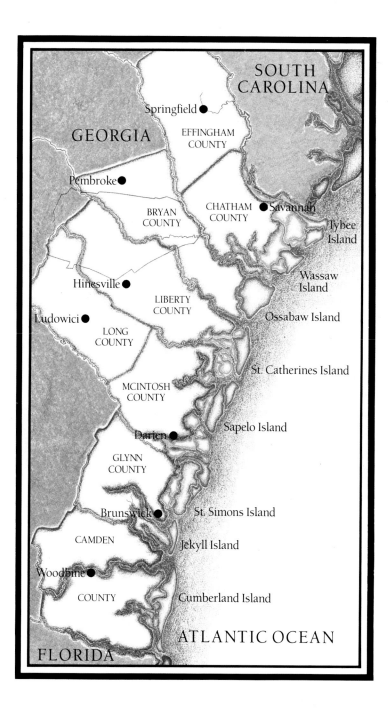

SOUTH CAROLINA

GEORGIA

Springfield ●

EFFINGHAM COUNTY

Pembroke ●

BRYAN COUNTY

CHATHAM COUNTY ● Savannah

Tybee Island

Hinesville ●

LIBERTY COUNTY

Wassaw Island

Ludowici ●

LONG COUNTY

Ossabaw Island

St. Catherines Island

MCINTOSH COUNTY

Darien ●

Sapelo Island

GLYNN COUNTY

Brunswick ●

St. Simons Island

CAMDEN

Jekyll Island

Woodbine ●

COUNTY

Cumberland Island

ATLANTIC OCEAN

FLORIDA

Chatham, Effingham and Bryan Counties

Historic Savannah

EFFINGHAM COUNTY

21

119

U.S. 17

37.

Springfield

Ebenezer Creek

97.

32

275

33.

Guyton

Rincon

I-95

GEORGIA

SOUTH
CAROLINA

U.S. 80

Pembroke

280

BRYAN COUNTY

Savannah River

119

I-16

26

83.

67

122.

U.S. 17

Savannah

82.

123

84

22
119

FORT STEWART

Canoochee River

129.

Tybee Island

CHATHAM COUNTY

144

128

42. 130

Williamson Island

Flemington

Wassaw Island
National Wildlife Refuge

196

Hinesville

Midway

81

Walthourville

38

Dorchester

7

U.S. 82

Riceboro

Sunbury

8.

Ossabaw Island

Ludowici

U.S. 25

19.

Medway River

ATLANTIC OCEAN

Liberty, Long and McIntosh Counties

17. Shell ring, ca. 1,500 B.C., Sapelo Island
20. Site of Fort King George, 1721, Darien
21. Baldcypress, Lewis Island
26. Vernon Square, Darien
36. Jones Creek Baptist Church, 1856, organized 1810, near Ludowici
44. Slave cabin, ca. 1820, Sapelo Island
45. Midway Church, 1792, Midway
46. Gwinnett House, ca. 1765, St. Catherines Island
47. Swamp, Long County
55. Bulltown Swamp, Woodmanston, Liberty County
57. Rice mill stack, ca. 1820, Butler Island, McIntosh County
59. Dike at abandoned rice field, Riceboro
63. Midway River, Sunbury
64. Fort Morris, ca. 1756, Sunbury
65. Sunbury Cemetery
68. Midway Church, 1792, Midway
69. Dorchester Presbyterian Church, 1854, Dorchester
70. Flemington Presbyterian Church, 1852, Flemington
71. Walthourville Presbyterian Church, 1884, Walthourville
85. Bacon-Fraser House, 1839, Hinesville
89. St. Cyprians Episcopal Church, 1876, Darien
99. Well Pavilion, 1907, Ludowici
102. Downey House, 1882, The Ridge, near Darien
120. Gould Cemetery, Harris Neck, McIntosh County
121. Taylors Creek Cemetery, Liberty County

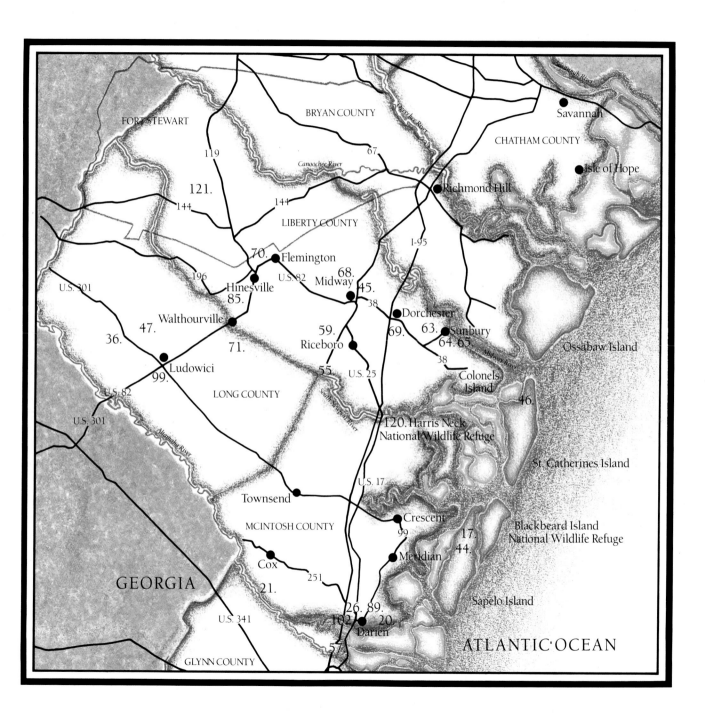

FORT STEWART

BRYAN COUNTY

Ogeechee River

Savannah

CHATHAM COUNTY

119

Canoochee River

67

121.

CHATHAM COUNTY

Isle of Hope

144

144

Richmond Hill

LIBERTY COUNTY

I-95

70.

Flemington

196

68.

85.

U.S. 82

Midway

45.

U.S. 301

Hinesville

38

Walthourville

Dorchester

47.

36.

71.

59.

Riceboro

69.

63.

Sunbury

64. 65.

Ossabaw Island

99.

Ludowici

55.

U.S. 25

38

LONG COUNTY

Colonels
Island

U.S. 82

South Newport River

46.

U.S. 301

Altamaha River

120. Harris Neck
National Wildlife Refuge

St. Catherines Island

U.S. 17

Townsend

MCINTOSH COUNTY

Crescent

99

17.

44.

Blackbeard Island
National Wildlife Refuge

Cox

251

Meridian

21.

Sapelo Island

GEORGIA

U.S. 341

26. 89.

102.

20.

57.

Darien

ATLANTIC OCEAN

GLYNN COUNTY

Glynn and Camden Counties

Cox

Meridian

251

90

Sapelo Island

Darien

Altamaha River

U.S. 341

56.
58.

32

38.
39.

GLYNN COUNTY

Little St. Simons Island

U.S. 25

108.

100.

118.

U.S. 84

80. 101.

Sea Island

40.

GEORGIA

107.

132.

St. Simons Island

115.

25.

78. 79.

Brunswick

127.

43.

Jekyll Island

U.S. 17

50.

I-95

114.
113.
112.

252

136.

Woodbine

Satilla River

Burnt Fort

2. Little Cumberland Island

CAMDEN COUNTY

Cumberland Island
National Seashore

40

St. Marys River

40

Kingsland

KINGS BAY

FLORIDA

41.

ATLANTIC OCEAN

110.
111.

St. Marys

66. 77.
67. 77.

SOURCES

Note: The sources for the quoted material in the pictorial section are designated by bracketed page numbers. The page numbers refer to their location in *Coastal Georgia*.

Bach, Bob, and Ginger Mercer, ed.. *Our Huckleberry Friend,* Secaucus, N. J.: Lyle Stuart, 1982. [104]

Bailey, Eloise, ed. *Camden's Challenge: A History of Camden County Georgia,* Woodbine: Camden County Historical Society, 1979. [64]

_____ and Virginia Proctor, ed. *Camden County Georgia,* Camden County Historical Commission, 1972.

_____. *Historical St. Marys Georgia,* St. Marys: St. Marys Chamber of Commerce, 1974.

Barnwell, Col. John. "Journal of Col. John Barnwell in the Construction of the Fort on the Altamaha in 1721." *South Carolina Historical Quarterly and Geneological Magazine,* Vol. 27 (1926). [32]

Bartram, William. *Travels Through North and South Carolina, Georgia, East and West Florida,* London: 1792, reprinted Savannah: The Beehive Press, 1973. [28, 54]

Bell, Malcolm, Jr.. *Savannah,* Savannah: Historic Savannah Foundation, 1977.

Bond, Mary Ion Wragg. *Personal Memoire of Savannah's Occupation,* a typescript in the library of Beth Lattimore Reiter.

Cate, Margaret Davis. *Early Days of Coastal Georgia,* St. Simons Island: Fort Frederica Association, 1955.

_____. *Our Todays and Yesterdays,* Brunswick: Glover Bros., 1930, reprinted Spartanburg, S. C.: The Reprint Co., 1979. [72, 88]

Cloues, Richard. "Guyton-Whitesville Historic District," Washington, D. C.: National Register of Historic Places, 1982.

_____. "Fort Screven Historic District," National Register of Historic Places, 1980.

Coulter, E. Merton. *Wormsloe, Two Centuries of a Georgia Family,* Wormsloe Foundation Publications, Athens: University of Georgia Press, 1955.

Drago, Edmund L.. *Black Politicians and Reconstruction in Georgia,* Baton Rouge: Louisiana State University Press, 1982.

Evans, Virginia Fraser, ed.. *Liberty County Georgia, A Pictorial History,* Statesville, North Carolina: Liberty County Board of Commissioners, 1979. [78]

Garden Club of Georgia. *Master Plan for the LeConte-Woodmanston Project,* 1981. [56, 72]

Georgia Writers' Project. *Drums and Shadows,* Garden City, New York: Anchor Books, Doubleday and Company, Inc., 1972.

Graham, Abbie Fuller. *Old Mill Days,* St. Simons Island: St. Simons Public Library, 1976. [74, 86]

Gunn, Victoria Reeves. *Hofwyl Plantation,* Atlanta: Department of Natural Resources, Office of Planning and Research, Historic Preservation, 1975.

Hanie, Robert. *Guale, the Golden Coast of Georgia,* San Francisco: Friends of the Earth, 1974. [24]

Harris, Joel Chandler. *Stories of Georgia,* New York: The American Book Co., [1896]. [52]

Hartridge, Walter C. *The Letters of Robert MacKay to His Wife,* Athens: University of Georgia Press, 1949.

_____. *The Letters of Don Juan McQueen to His Family,* Columbia, S. C.: Bostick & Thornley, 1943.

_____, and Christopher Murphy, Jr.. *Savannah,* Columbia: Bostick & Thornley, 1947.

Hazzard, Thomas Fuller. "The Culture of Flowers as Conducive to Health, Pleasure, and Rational Amusement." *Southern Agriculturist* Vol. 5, No. 10 (1832): pp. 513.

Holland, James W. "The Beginning of Public Agriculture Experimentation in America." *Agricultural History* 12: (July, 1938). pp. 271-298.

Hvidt, Kristian, ed.. *Von Reck's Voyage,* Savannah: The Beehive Press, 1980. [28, 42]

Jackson, Harvey, H. and Phinizy Spalding. *Forty Years of Diversity, Essays on Colonial Georgia,* Athens: University of Georgia Press, 1984.

Jones, Charles Colcock, Jr. *The History of Georgia,* Vols. I and II, Boston: Houghton, Mifflin and Company, 1883. [30, 34, 36, 38, 42, 46, 50]

_____. *The Dead Towns of Georgia,* Savannah: 1878, reprinted in Atlanta: Cherokee Publishing Co., 1974. [62]

Kemble, Frances Anne. *Journal of a Residence on a Georgian Plantation in 1838-1839,* New York: Harper and Bros., 1863. [58]

Lane, Mills. *The People of Georgia,* Savannah: Beehive Press, 1975.

_____, ed.. *The Rambler in Georgia,* Savannah: The Beehive Press, 1973.

Lanier, Charles. *Jekyll Island Club,* Brunswick: 1916. [94]

Lawrence, Alexander A. *Storm Over Savannah,* Athens: The University of Georgia Press, 1951.

——————————. *A Present for Mr. Lincoln,* Macon: The Ardivan Press, Inc., 1961.

Lewis, Bessie. *They Called Their Town Darien,* Darien: The Darien News, 1975.

Lovell, Caroline Couper. *The Golden Isles of Georgia,* Boston: Little Brown and Co., 1932. [72]

Lyell, Charles. *A Second Visit to the United States of North America,* New York: 1849, as quoted in Mills Lane, ed. *The Rambler in Georgia,* Savannah: Beehive Press, 1973. [84]

McDonald, Susan. "Liberty, A Shockless Driving Tour of Georgia's Most History-Jammed County." *Brown's Guide to Georgia* p. 30 ff (February 1981).

McIlvaine, Paul. *The Dead Town of Sunbury, Georgia,* Asheville, N. C.: Groves Printing Co., 1971.

McKay, Frances Peabody. *More Fun Than Heaven,* St. Petersburg: Valkyrie Press, Inc., 1978. [100]

Martin, Harold H.. *This Happy Isle,* Sea Island: Sea Island Co., 1978.

Matlack, Carol. "Savannah." *American Preservation,* Vol. II, No. 3, (1979) pp. 9-25. [106]

Morrison, Mary L.. *Historic Savannah,* Savannah: Historic Savannah Foundation, 1979.

Myers, Robert Manson, ed.. *The Children of Pride,* New Haven and London: Yale University Press, 1972. [76]

Ober, Frederick A. *Dungeness, General Greene's Sea Island Plantation,* J. B. Lippincott Co., 1880. [92]

Potterfield, Ty. "D'Antignac House," National Register for Historic Places, copy at Coastal Area Planning and Development Commission (CAPDC).

——————. "Ridge Historic District," National Register for Historic Places, 1978, copy at CAPDC.

Reiter, Beth Lattimore. "Old Town Historic District," National Register for Historic Places, 1978, copy at CAPDC.

——————————. "Richmond Hill Plantation," National Register for Historic Places, 1977, copy at CAPDC.

——————————. "St. Simons—Sea Island Multiple Resource Nomination," National Register for Historic Places, 1982, copy at CAPDC.

Savannah Morning News, Savannah: 1869 [82]; October 14, 1873 [78]; August 29, 1880 [84]; April 14, 1940 [98]; May 30, 1940 [98]; November 10, 1940 [98]; 1938 columns of Thomas Gamble [80, 82]; January 26, 1957 [102]

Scarbrough, William. "Letter to Julia." William Scarbrough Collection, Atlanta: Georgia Department of Archives and History, May 6, 1819. [60]

Sheftall, Benjamin. "Diary of Benjamin Sheftall." *American Jewish Historical Quarterly,* Vol. LIV, No. 3 (1965).

Spalding, Thomas. "On the Mode of Constructing Tabby Buildings, and the propriety of improving our plantations in a permanent manner." *The Southern Agriculturist,* Vol. III, No. 12 (1830), pp. 617-623. [48]

Smith, R. L., et al. "Archaeological Survey and Testing at Hunter Army Airfield," 1984, copy at Armstrong State College History Department.

Smith, Joseph W. *Visits to Brunswick Georgia and Travels South,* Andover, Mass.: 1907. [90]

Stacy, Dr. James. *History of the Midway Congregational Church,* Newnan, Ga.: 1903, reprinted 1951. [66]

Stevens, The Rev. William Baker, M. D.. *A History of Georgia,* Vol. 1, New York: D. Appleton and Co., 1847. [44]

Thackeray, William Makepeace. *A Collection of Letters of Thackeray,* New York: Charles Scribner and Sons, 1887. [70]

Van Story, Burnette. *Georgia's Land of the Golden Isles,* Athens: The University of Georgia Press, 1956 (Revised edition, 1970).

Waring, Antonio J., Jr. (Stepen Williams, ed.) *The Waring Papers: The Southern Cult,* Athens: The University of Georgia Press, 1967.